**NATIONAL
GEOGRAPHIC
KiDS**

SPACE
ENCYCLOPEDIA

A TOUR OF OUR SOLAR SYSTEM AND BEYOND

WRITTEN & ILLUSTRATED BY DAVID A. AGUILAR

CONTRIBUTING WRITERS
CHRISTINE PULLIAM & PATRICIA DANIELS

NATIONAL GEOGRAPHIC
WASHINGTON, D.C.

TABLE OF CONTENTS

Introduction by David A. Aguilar **6**

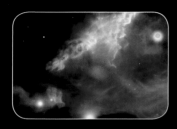

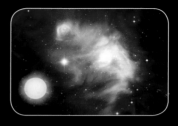

Art preceding pages: Page 1, A decorative composite of a planet, star, and galaxy; Pages 2–3, An alien world and its moon in the heart of the Milky Way

In the "To the Stars & Beyond" chapter, when a picture of a constellation, galaxy, or nebula has the binocular symbol beside it, that means you can use your own binoculars to look for the object in the night sky.

ABOUT THE ILLUSTRATIONS

The art for this book was created by David A. Aguilar on his computer. He began by gathering the best scientific information available. Using that information, he sketched images that were as realistic as possible in his notebook. Then he transferred those sketches to his computer and painted with his mouse, using Adobe Photoshop and building up layer on layer, until his vision of space appeared. Sometimes he built models of spaceships out of junk plastic found around his house (again using the latest data to guide his hand). Or he made planetary landscapes out of torn pieces of paper towels dipped into watered-down plaster of paris, then photographed them and colored them in Photoshop. In some cases he also incorporated images taken by telescopes and satellites into the art. Why do we even need artwork in a book about the real world? Sometimes we don't. For example, we have very good photographs of Mars, but there are many other places (such as extra-solar planets) and many perspectives (such as gazing at Jupiter from the surface of Europa) and possible future events (such as astronauts visiting Uranus's moon Miranda) that we can only visualize by turning scientific data into art. Some of these imaginary images will never actually be seen, because no telescope is capable of photographing them.

The photographs in this book were taken by satellites and telescopes, as well as by cameras here on Earth. Most came from NASA, the National Aeronautics and Space Administration.

Growing up in the Santa Clara Valley in California, I lived in a dreamland for anyone in love with nature. Orchards full of quail and pheasant stretched as far as a young person could hike in a day. The white, pink, and blue blossoms of fruit trees filled the air when gentle breezes blew in from the Pacific Ocean. Half an hour away, tide pools and clear cold waters awaited the young underwater explorer. It was a nature lover's paradise.

My bedroom was filled with insect collections, pressed wildflowers, fossils, terrariums, and model airplanes. On the walls were posters and drawings of planets and galaxies, and in the corner stood my trusty three-inch reflecting telescope, which I constructed all by myself (photo-illustration at right).

For the mirror of my telescope, I had used two glass casters "borrowed" from my grandmother's four-poster bed. The casters were like small glass cups that people used to put beneath the legs of their beds so that the legs wouldn't scratch the floor. I had ground the casters together with abrasives purchased from a rock shop, then polished them using a mixture of water and jeweler's rouge on top of sticky pitch collected from our cherry tree.

My eyepiece was constructed from two slightly chipped lenses salvaged from the pirate spyglass my brother bought at the county fair. I glued the lenses inside the plastic top of a mouthwash bottle. My cardboard telescope tube came from the trash bin behind a carpet store, and my mount was made from scrap lumber and a few inexpensive plumbers pipe fittings. A little paint here and there, and I was in business exploring the universe.

My telescope worked better than anything Galileo used to make his discoveries. I named it Mable, after my grandmother.

The first thing I looked at was the moon. I saw craters, flat valleys, and mountains everywhere! Seeing the moons of Jupiter and the rings of Saturn opened my eyes and imagination in ways I had never experienced before. Little did I know that my hobby would someday become my career.

Besides telescopes, there was something else that drew me to astronomy. It was the mystery of UFOs. In my young mind the same question kept popping up: What if they are real? What if they really are out there?

Today, I am part of one of the largest astronomical research organizations in the world—the Harvard-Smithsonian Center for Astrophysics. Our observatories are located on mountaintops in Chile, Arizona, and Hawaii and in orbit above our heads in space. When I come to work each morning, I never know what great discovery may await me.

The discoveries astronomers make sometimes change the way we think about ourselves and our place in the universe. In the next 25 years we may know the answers to these really big questions: What caused the big bang? What invisible force is speeding up the expansion of the universe? Are there other universes out there besides our own? What type of life exists on other planets? Are there other "Earth-worlds" out there? And maybe, once and for all, what is this phenomenon we call UFOs all about?

This is why I love astronomy so much. The biggest questions regarding our universe are waiting to be answered. Somewhere out there in the world today are the future scientists who will find the answers to these great questions. Maybe one of them will be you.

DAVID A. AGUILAR

After the big bang that gave rise to our universe, stars began to form from clouds of gas and dust.

WHAT WE KNOW

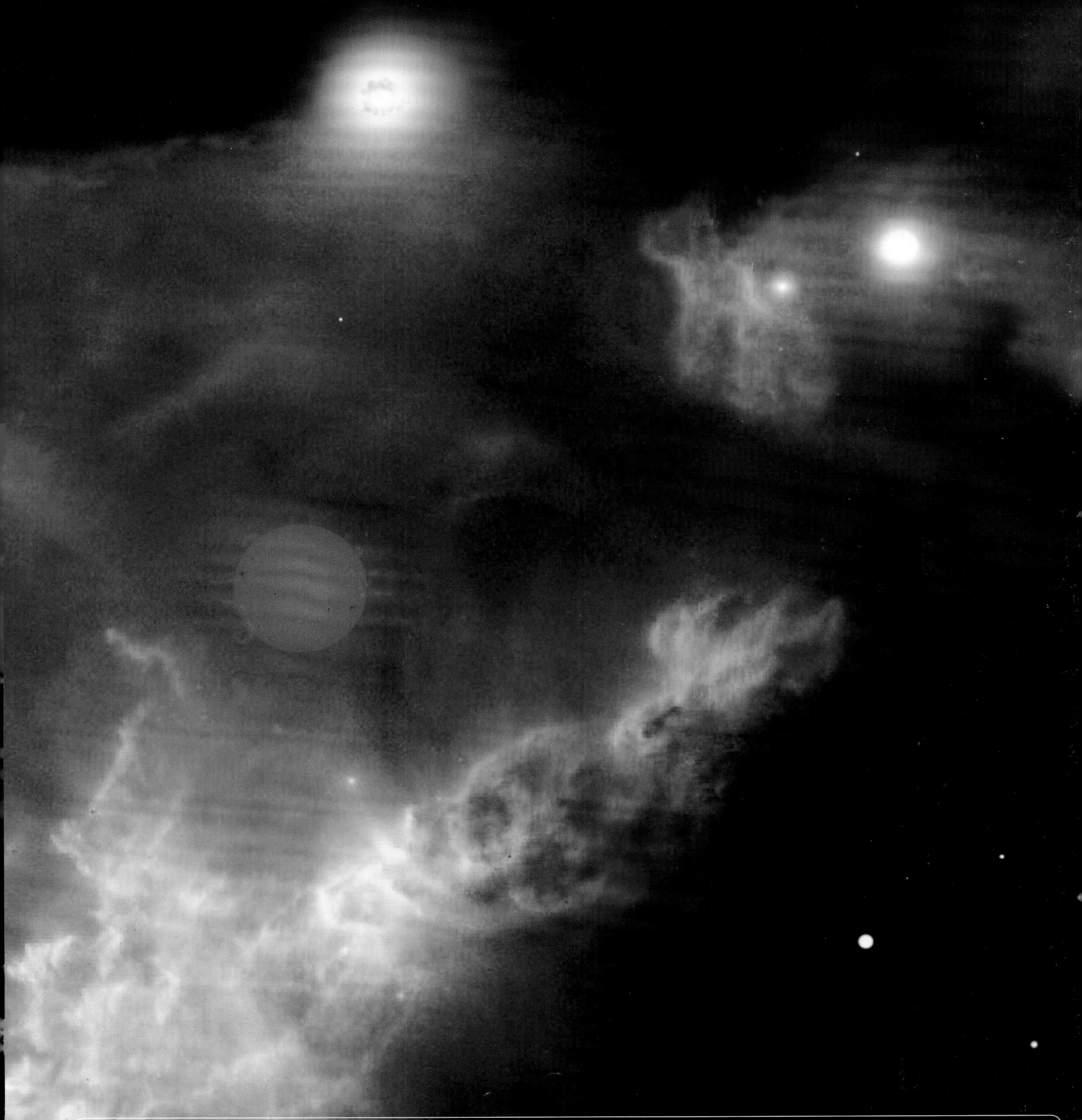

Clear your mind for a minute and try to imagine this: All the things you see in the universe today—all the stars, galaxies, and planets floating around out there—do not exist. Everything that now exists is concentrated in a single, incredibly dense point scientists call a singularity. Then, suddenly, the elements that make the material universe flash into existence. That actually happened about 13.7 billion years ago, in the moment we call the big bang.

For centuries scientists, religious scholars, poets, and philosophers wondered how the universe came to be. Was it always there? Will it always be the same, or will it change? If it had a beginning, will it someday end, or will it go on forever?

These were huge questions. But today, because of our recent observations of space and what it's made of, we think we may have answers to some of them. We know the big bang created not only matter but space itself. We also think in the very distant future stars will run out of fuel and blink out. Once again the universe will become dark.

Everything we can see or detect around us in the universe began with the big bang. It wasn't a violent explosion like a stick of dynamite blowing up. Instead, it was like a giant balloon inflating.

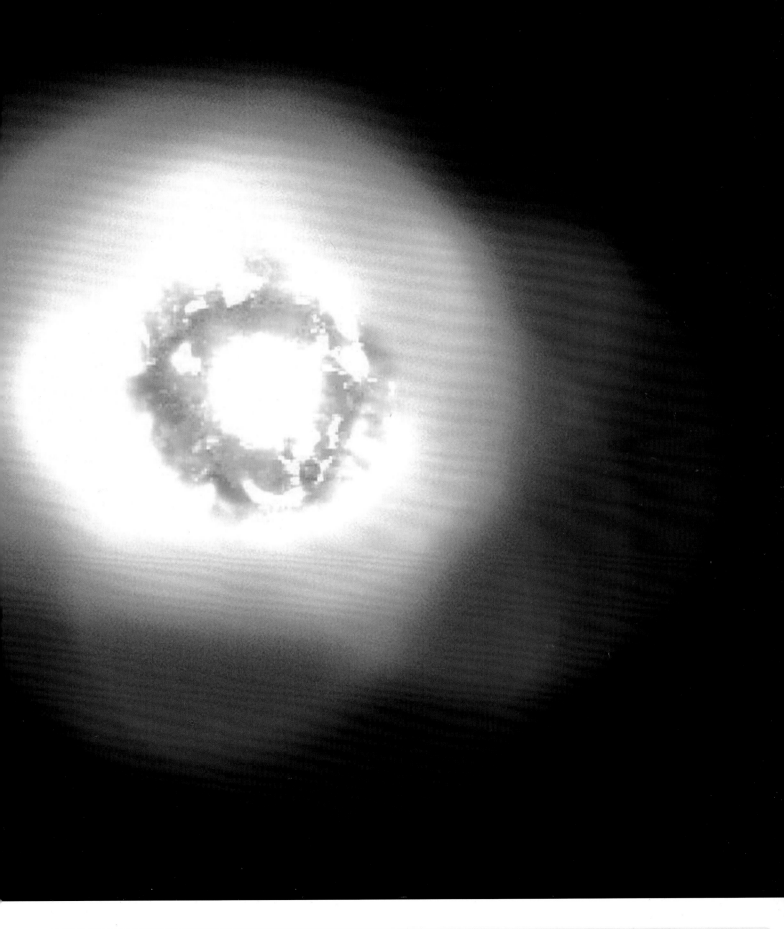

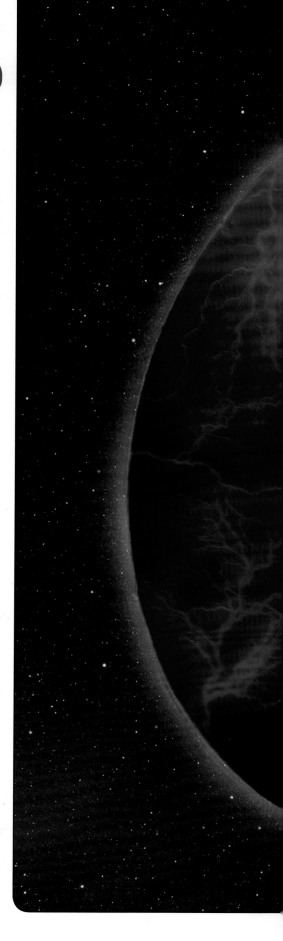

Astronomers have learned that there's a lot more to the universe than what we can see directly. It's like an iceberg. The part of the iceberg that's visible floating above the surface is only one-tenth of all the ice. The other nine-tenths lurks underwater, unseen.

In our universe, the gas, stars, and galaxies we can see make up about 4 percent of what is out there. We know there's more we can't see because the unseen "stuff" exerts a gravitational force. It pulls on the stuff we can see. But gravity provides our only clue. The unseen stuff doesn't emit radiation that we can detect, so astronomers call it dark matter.

What is dark matter made of? We don't know. It's not just dark stars or planets or even black holes. It may be vast numbers of tiny particles. We do know that, whatever it is, it makes up about 23 percent of the universe.

DARK ENERGY

So if regular matter and dark matter together are about 27 percent of the universe, what makes up the other 73 percent? An even more mysterious thing called dark energy. Until the late 1990s, we didn't even know it existed. Then astronomers discovered, to their amazement, that the universe was not only expanding, but speeding up as it expanded.

We still don't know the source of the energy that is powering this speed. Is it some new kind of energy field, or a property of space itself? Or are we completely mistaken about some basic facts of physics and gravity? Will dark energy make physicists rewrite the laws of physics in order to understand the universe? One thing we do know: the universe is much stranger than we ever imagined.

A mysterious material called dark matter surrounds all the galaxies in the universe, holding them together and keeping them from flying apart. Another force called dark energy is doing the opposite—pushing everything in the universe apart. Combined, dark matter and dark energy make up 96 percent of our universe. Both are invisible to us.

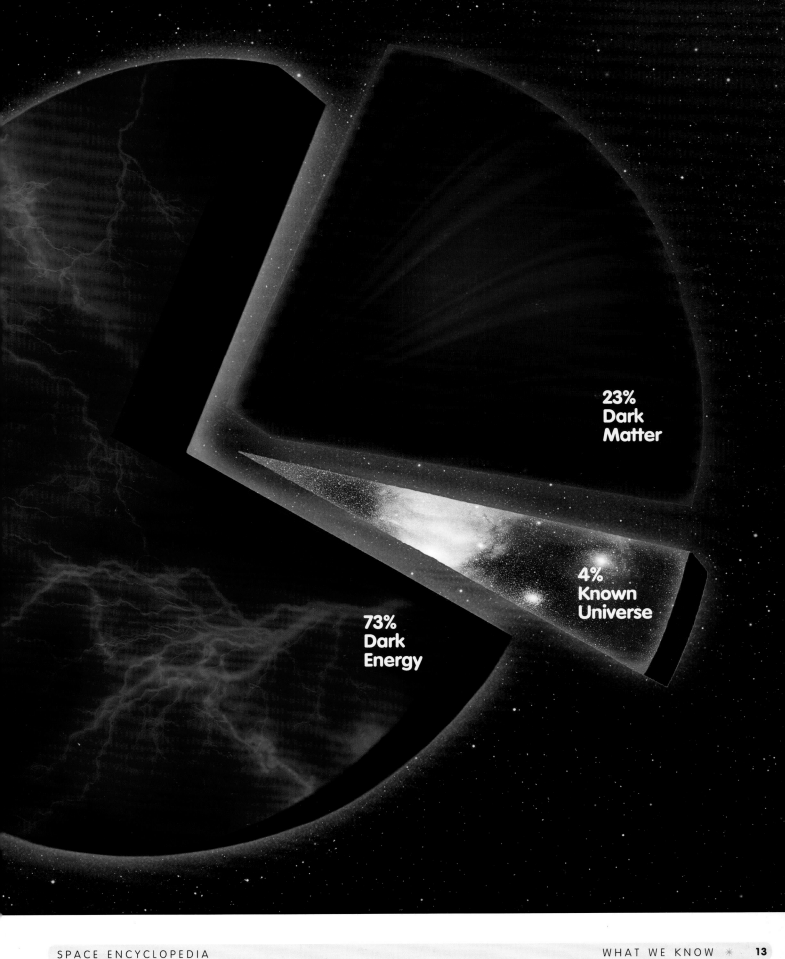

23%
Dark
Matter

4%
Known
Universe

73%
Dark
Energy

Humans long believed that there were other planets out in space, circling around distant stars. Scientists just never knew where to look for them. In the past 20 years all that has changed. Today, astronomers have confirmed more than 900 extra-solar (outside of our solar system) planets, and the number continues to climb. Some astronomers think that there are at least 100 billion planets in our galaxy alone.

These planets come in a variety of sizes, temperatures, and orbits. Many detected so far are giants like Jupiter and Saturn—but this is mostly because these are easier to spot. Big observatories on Earth and orbiting telescopes have also found small, rocky planets, boiling hot planets, iceball planets, systems with nine planets, planets around double stars, planets around red giant stars, and even lonely wandering planets without a star.

The great prize for planet-finders, though, will be an Earthlike, Earth-size planet in the "habitable zone." This is an orbit that keeps a planet warm enough to hold liquid water on its surface—and maybe to host life. Scientists are now beginning to identify some candidates. Will there be life on them? Stay tuned!

The newly discovered planets Kepler 62e and f are Earth-size worlds in the habitable zone of a distant sunlike star. The larger planet (upper right), Kepler f, is farthest from its star and covered by ice. Kepler e, shown with its rings, is nearer to its star and covered by dense clouds. Both planets may be capable of supporting life.

Have you ever caught the bright flash of a meteor streaking across the night sky? It was probably a piece of space debris not much larger than a pencil eraser. Every day, the Earth gains about a hundred tons from that kind of debris raining down on it.

Most of it is no bigger than a lemon, but not all. About 180 impact craters have been identified on Earth, created by falling objects larger than a house.

In 1908, in the air above a forest in the Tunguska region of Siberia, something exploded, flattening 80 million trees over an area of 830 square miles (2,150 sq km). Some 50,000 years ago, a meteor hit the desert in what is now northern Arizona, creating the Barringer Crater. It's one mile (1.6 km) in diameter and 570 feet (170 m) deep.

The most dazzling collision, however, came 65 million years ago, when a very large asteroid struck off the eastern coast of Mexico. That spectacular event changed global weather. Some scientists think the change in climate eventually led to the extinction of the dinosaurs.

We didn't have telescopes watching the Earth when these big impacts happened. But in recent years we have seen comets and asteroids smack into the solar system's biggest planet, Jupiter. In 1992, for instance, a comet named Shoemaker-Levy 9 was torn to bits by Jupiter's powerful gravitational field. In July 1994, those orbiting pieces took their revenge. Chunks up to 1.2 miles (2 km) wide rained down into Jupiter's atmosphere like enormous bombs. They caused giant fireballs, and some left dark clouds of debris the size of planets. Another such collision happened in 2009, when an object—maybe an asteroid—plowed into Jupiter with a force thousands of times greater than Earth's Tunguska blast.

Jupiter may protect the Earth from some comet collisions by snaring these objects before they reach us. However, traveling asteroids and comets are still a danger to our planet. Several space agencies now track these Near-Earth Objects, planning for the day when we may have to defend ourselves against the next big impact.

A 5000°F (2760°C) fireball four miles (6.5 km) in diameter slams through our atmosphere (art left), its blinding light a hundred times brighter than the sun. Could Earth get hit by an asteroid? Yes. More than 250 near-Earth asteroids cross our orbital path. Many have the potential to collide with us in the future.

Our planet has its own atmosphere and its own weather, from calm to stormy. The Earth lives in the light of the sun. The sun, too, has weather, and its storms can affect our world.

The sun is constantly giving off both radiation and the solar wind. We feel the radiation mostly as life-giving warmth. Our atmosphere blocks most of the dangerous radiation, the kind that can give us cancer if we aren't protected.

Some of the sun's hot outer atmosphere, its corona, escapes into space in the form of electrically charged particles. This is the solar wind. The sun sheds millions of tons of its gas this way every second—but because the sun is so huge, this loss doesn't matter to it.

When the solar wind reaches the Earth, it is usually deflected by our planet's magnetic field. Sometimes its particles enter the magnetic field and create beautiful, shimmering auroras in the polar skies.

SOLAR STORMS

While the sun's heat is always steady, its blasts of charged particles can change from hour to hour. Active magnetic regions on the sun sometimes shoot out solar flares or clouds of magnetized gas called coronal mass ejections (CMEs). These explosions of solar gases contain high-energy radiation and charged particles.

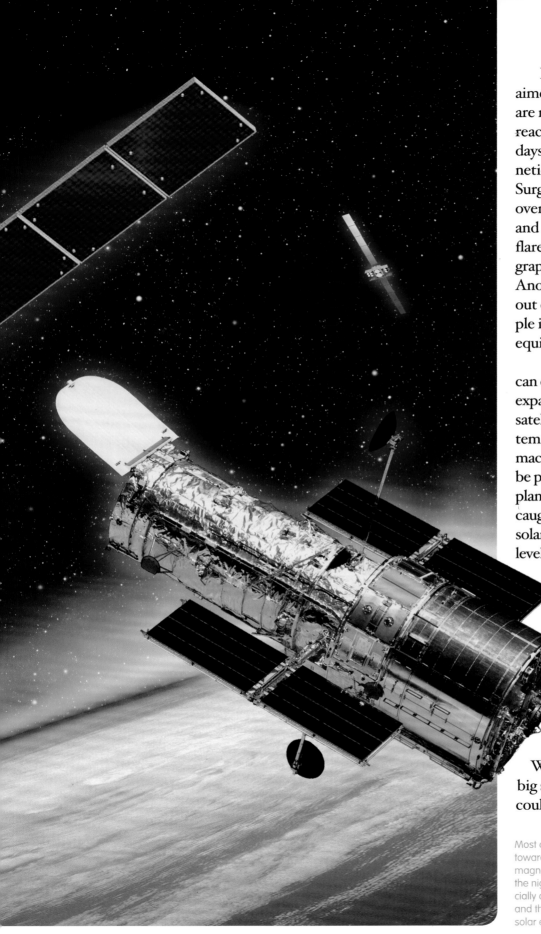

If these flares or CMEs are aimed toward Earth (and most are not), their charged particles reach our atmosphere in several days. The effects of these magnetic solar storms can be serious. Surges in electrical energy can overload transformers on Earth and cause blackouts. A giant solar flare in 1859 knocked out telegraph systems around the world. Another storm in 1989 blacked out electricity for six million people in Canada and melted power equipment in New Jersey.

Radiation from solar storms can cause our atmosphere to expand temporarily, dragging on satellites. Global positioning system (GPS) signals that guide our machinery can go awry. Flares can be particularly harmful to airplanes and spacecraft. Airplanes caught at high altitudes during a solar storm can be hit with high levels of radiation. Even worse can happen to spacecraft, unprotected by Earth's atmosphere. In 2002, the Mars spacecraft Nozomi was caught in a solar flare and broke down. Its mission had to be canceled. Some agencies now track and predict solar weather. Without advance warning, a big storm like the one in 1859 could shut us down.

Most of the radiation and energy directed toward the Earth from space is deflected by our magnetic field, resulting in beautiful auroras in the night skies. Satellites in orbit, however, especially communication satellites, can be disrupted and their electronics can be destroyed by these solar events we now call "space weather."

Since their invention in the 1600s, telescopes have shown that there is more to the universe than meets the eye. By magnifying the light of distant objects, telescopes can reveal previously unseen planets, stars, and galaxies. The first telescopes collected visible light, or light we can see with our eyes. By the 20th century, telescopes could track not only visible light, but also all kinds of invisible light, or radiation, such as radio waves, x-rays, and gamma rays.

To collect different types of radiation, astronomers build different kinds of telescopes. And when it comes to size, bigger is usually better. A big mirror or radio dish can collect more radiation than a small one. This gives astronomers more information to work with. So scientists are now building some of the biggest telescopes ever. The well-named Very Large Telescope (VLT), in Chile's Atacama Desert, has four telescopes with mirrors 27 feet (8.2 m) wide. Each telescope can be used by itself, or the four can work together to study the same object. When completed, the Giant Magellan Telescope (GMT) will also be located in the Atacama Desert. Its seven mirrors will have a combined working area 80 feet (24.5 m) across.

Joining these in the desert is the collection of radio telescopes known as the Atacama Large Millimeter/submillimeter Array, or ALMA. Signals from its 66 radio dishes will be combined by a computer to form one very strong signal. ALMA will look into areas of space too dark for regular telescopes.

The Thirty Meter Telescope (TMT) is not yet built. When it is complete on top of Hawaii's big mountain, Mauna Kea, its 98-foot (30-m)-wide mirror will pull in visible light as well as invisible infrared light from deep space.

By observing all forms of radiation, astronomers learn more about the universe than they could from studying visible light alone.

Three new major telescope projects, currently under way, will change our views of the universe. The Giant Magellan Telescope (left) and the Thirty Meter Telescope (right) will be completed in 2021. They will be the largest optical telescopes ever built. To be launched in 2018, the James Webb Space Telescope, shown here in orbit, will replace the Hubble Space Telescope. It will be the last of the great telescopes launched into space for many decades to come.

As our spaceship passes Neptune, the sunlight is bright, even though the sun is nearly three billion miles (4.8 billion km) away.

Ceres

Mars

Earth

Venus

Mercury

Jupiter

Sun

The solar system is made up of planets, asteroids, and comets orbiting around a star we call the sun. Our star system formed 4.6 billion years ago from a nebular cloud—a large, spinning cloud of gas and dust. Today, astronomers divide the solar system into three different categories of planets, based on their size and density. Orbiting closest to the sun are the small, dense, rocky worlds of Mercury, Venus, Earth, and Mars. If they were dropped into a gigantic tub of water, they would sink. We call them the terrestrial planets—a word taken from the Latin word *terra,* which means "land."

Beyond the terrestrial planets lies the asteroid belt, filled with small rocky asteroids and our fifth planet, Ceres. It's a dwarf planet, a category established in 2006 by the International Astronomical Union.

Next come the gas giants—Jupiter, Saturn, Uranus, and Neptune. They're large,

Saturn

Uranus

Neptune

Pluto

Haumea

Makemake

Eris

surrounded by rings and multiple moons, and made out of gases. Astronomers call them the Jovian planets, after the Roman god Jove, which is another name for Jupiter.

Past the gas giant planets, extending far out into space, is the Kuiper belt, an area filled with comets and other galactic debris. Also orbiting the sun in the Kuiper belt are Pluto; its moon, Charon; and our 13th planet, Eris. Like Ceres in the asteroid belt, Pluto and Eris are now classified as dwarf planets. They're made of a mixture of ice and rock. Following Pluto and Eris are our newest planets, Haumea and Makemake.

This artwork shows the 13 planets that astronomers now recognize in our solar system. The relative sizes of the planets are also shown, but not the relative distances between them or their true placements as they orbit the sun. Many of the planets, except the ones far from the sun, can be seen in the night sky without a telescope.

THE GRAND TOUR

Longer than most luxury cruise ships traveling Earth's oceans, our imaginary voyager, *Stella Nova*, which means "new star," will take us to the dwarf planet Eris in the farthest reaches of the solar system. Our crew consists of a captain, a chief pilot and navigator, a flight engineer, a medical doctor, two scientists, a payload specialist, and two lucky guests. The total number of crew members isn't much more than what was usually on board the space shuttle.

This will be mostly a sight-seeing and reconnaissance tour, so we'll spend a lot of time simply observing. Much of what needs to be done will be done by the computers on board the ship. Even the flight plan is locked in, so *Stella Nova* will more or less fly itself. That's good, because whatever we try to do, from work to

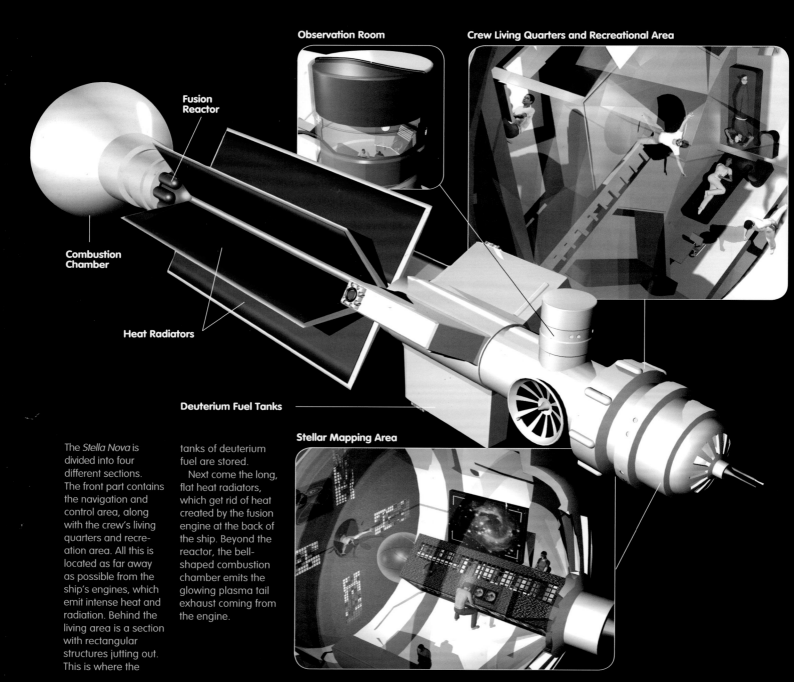

Observation Room

Crew Living Quarters and Recreational Area

Fusion Reactor

Combustion Chamber

Heat Radiators

Deuterium Fuel Tanks

Stellar Mapping Area

The *Stella Nova* is divided into four different sections. The front part contains the navigation and control area, along with the crew's living quarters and recreation area. All this is located as far away as possible from the ship's engines, which emit intense heat and radiation. Behind the living area is a section with rectangular structures jutting out. This is where the tanks of deuterium fuel are stored.

Next come the long, flat heat radiators, which get rid of heat created by the fusion engine at the back of the ship. Beyond the reactor, the bell-shaped combustion chamber emits the glowing plasma tail exhaust coming from the engine.

exercise, we'll have to do in zero gravity, which means we'll be floating through *Stella Nova* as we speed through space.

MOVING FAST

Our journey to the most distant planet now known will take only months instead of years, because our spaceship is powered by nuclear fusion. The nuclear reactor on board fuses deuterium, also called heavy hydrogen, and helium-3. This allows us to travel incredibly fast—at one percent the speed of light. Light travels at about 186,000 miles (300,000 km) per second, so we'll be zooming along at more than 600 million miles (966 million km) per hour. At that speed we can journey out to Eris and be back on Earth in just 60 days. By comparison, the space shuttle poked along at 17,500 miles (28,164 km) per hour, so the same trip, without any stops, would take more than 70 years to complete.

Although the idea of a fusion-powered ship is already scientifically possible, building one isn't practical yet. We still need to develop the technology to contain the heat and radiation that fusion would generate. Scientists are working on this challenge right now.

Our flight will take us in toward the sun before we zoom out to the planets beyond Earth. We planned it that way to take advantage of something called "gravitational assist." This is how it works: We aim the ship at a particular angle when approaching a planet or the sun. Gravity pulls us into that object's orbit, so we both accelerate and save on fuel. Passing the planet, we spin out of its orbit and shoot into space as if hurled by a giant slingshot. Many satellites already use this method to speed along.

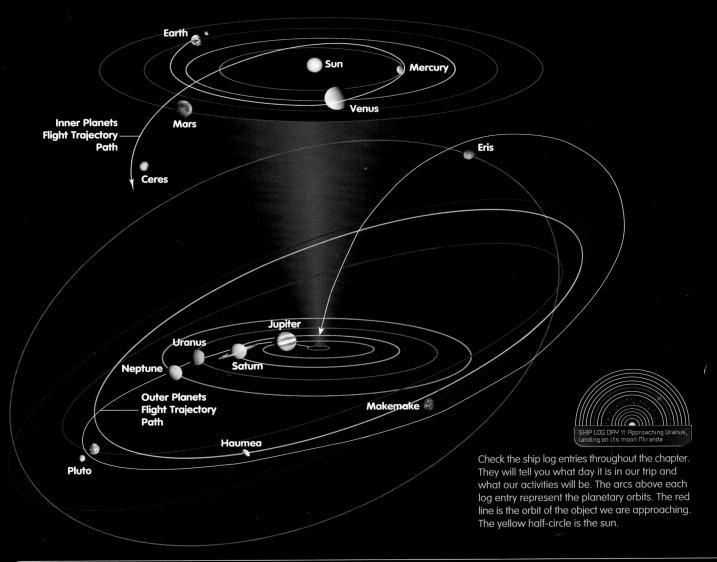

Check the ship log entries throughout the chapter. They will tell you what day it is in our trip and what our activities will be. The arcs above each log entry represent the planetary orbits. The red line is the orbit of the object we are approaching. The yellow half-circle is the sun.

V E N U S

Shining like a brilliant jewel in space, Venus has been called Earth's sister planet. Despite the fact that humans like to associate it with things of beauty, Venus has an eerie red landscape with thick clouds that choke out the sunlight.

Slightly smaller than Earth, Venus has a chemical composition similar to Earth's. In the past it may have been covered by oceans and may have had a moon. But today Venus is one of the most inhospitable planets in the solar system.

Blanketed in a cloud layer of carbon dioxide 40 miles (64 km) thick, Venus has the densest atmosphere of any planet in the solar system, 90 times denser than Earth's atmosphere. Anyone venturing out onto the surface would be crushed like a paper cup—or toasted.

Venus's surface temperatures reach 880°F (471°C)—hot enough to melt lead. At the top of its clouds, winds roar at more than 200 miles (320 km) per hour. On the surface, though, the wind hardly blows. But the air has so much density that even a gentle breeze would push you along like a large ocean wave.

SHIP LOG 8 HOURS: Approaching Venus, radar reconnaissance of volcanism

FACTS ABOUT VENUS	
AVERAGE DISTANCE FROM THE SUN	67,238,251 MILES (108,209,475 KM)
POSITION FROM THE SUN IN ORBIT	SECOND
EQUATORIAL DIAMETER	7,520 MILES (12,100 KM)
MASS (EARTH = 1)	0.815
DENSITY (WATER = 1)	5.24
LENGTH OF DAY	243 EARTH DAYS
LENGTH OF YEAR	225 EARTH DAYS
AVERAGE SURFACE TEMPERATURE	880°F (471°C)
KNOWN MOONS	0

Earth

Venus

As our spaceship approaches Venus (art right), the planet's golden crescent shines brilliantly because its clouds reflect sunlight back into space. Beyond Venus, the stars of the Pleiades constellation, also called the Seven Sisters, sparkle in the sky.

Until the late 1950s, scientists believed Venus was a world covered by swamps and lush tropical jungles. Today, we know it doesn't look like that at all. Venus is one of the driest places in the solar system, with no trace of water. No need for weather predicting here. As far as astronomers can tell, rain never occurs. Falling droplets of sulfuric acid evaporate before they reach the ground. The temperature doesn't change between day and night. It is the same forecast all the time.

Venus's surface is pocked by large meteor craters that range in size from 1.5 miles to 170 miles (2.4 to 270 km) across. There are no small craters because the thick atmosphere causes smaller meteorites to burn up before hitting the ground. Two large, flat highland areas may have been left behind from an earlier time, when there were ancient oceans on Venus. One in the northern hemisphere, Ishtar Terra, is about the size of Australia. Along the equator, Aphrodite Terra is about the size of South America.

A VOLCANIC WORLD

Volcanoes of every size and type rise from the planet's vast plains, and much of Venus is covered by lava. Almost 170 of these volcanoes are

Core: nickel-iron
Mantle: silicates
Crust: silicates

Like Earth, Venus has a nickel-iron core surrounded by a molten-rock mantle and crust. As this mantle of molten rock pushed up, it flowed out of volcanoes in the form of lava. The oldest surface features on Venus are less than 800 million years old.

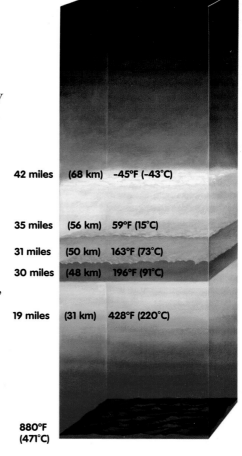

42 miles	(68 km)	-45°F (-43°C)
35 miles	(56 km)	59°F (15°C)
31 miles	(50 km)	163°F (73°C)
30 miles	(48 km)	196°F (91°C)
19 miles	(31 km)	428°F (220°C)
880°F (471°C)		

Clouds form a thick blanket around Venus (art above), reflecting sunlight back into space and keeping the planet much cooler than it would be without them. But the high concentration of carbon dioxide in the atmosphere also traps heat, causing the greenhouse effect. Scientists are now concerned about the growing concentration of carbon dioxide in Earth's atmosphere.

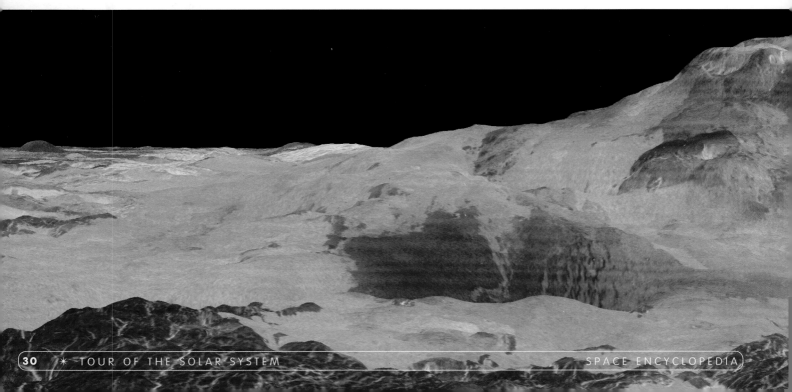

more than 60 miles (97 km) wide.

The tremendous heat on Venus was the result of volcanic eruptions that released carbon dioxide into the atmosphere, creating the greenhouse effect. Scientists think rising temperatures caused Venus's ancient oceans to evaporate.

Some day, hundreds of millions of years from now, when the volcanic eruptions are far in the past, Venus will begin to cool, and oceans may form. They will help speed up the removal of carbon dioxide from the atmosphere by naturally dissolving it into the seawater, just as oceans do here on Earth. Venus may then be more Earthlike and become our true twin sister.

The landscape of Venus is 80 percent volcanic plains covered by strange dome-like structures that are the result of molten rock bulging out, then hardening. The shield volcano known as Gula Mons (art below) stands about 2.4 miles (4 km) high.

PHASES OF VENUS

Venus is the third brightest object in our sky, after the sun and moon. In fact, if you have a star chart and know where to look in the sky, you can spot Venus even in the daytime. The ancient Greeks believed it was two separate objects: Hersperus, the evening star, and Phosphorus, the morning star. Because its orbit is inside the Earth's, Venus can appear in both the early evening sky and the early morning sky.

Viewed from Earth, Venus goes through phase changes (art above), just like the moon. When it is farthest away from us in its orbit, it looks smallest in size but is fully illuminated by the sun. In shape it resembles a full moon. As it draws nearer to Earth, its size grows larger but its phase now resembles a thin crescent, so it looks dimmer to us.

When the astronomer Galileo first observed Venus in 1610, it was added proof that not everything in the heavens circled around Earth, as many believed. Galileo's observation was important evidence for the theory that Earth—and all the other planets—circled around the sun.

You can easily watch Venus change phases over a period of weeks with a small telescope at 40x. It may appear slightly distorted, with rings of yellow and purple around it, because our thick atmosphere distorts light from Venus.

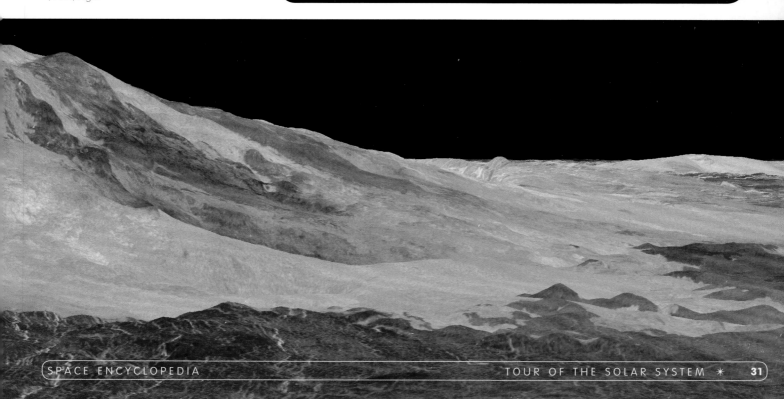

M E R C U R Y

SHIP LOG 17 HOURS: Landing on Mercury, replace seismic monitors

The next planet on our tour is Mercury, the innermost and smallest of the rocky planets. Because it orbits so close to the sun, this planet is usually lost in the sun's glare and difficult to see from Earth. The terrain is scarred with craters, high ragged walls, and old volcanoes. The rims of barely visible "ghost craters" are buried under volcanic rock from a time when lava flooded the surface.

Mercury's axis doesn't tilt, so the sun shines directly on the equator, making it sizzling hot during the day and freezing cold at night. Temperatures can range from 800°F (427°C) in the sunlight to –279°F (–173°C) on the night side. Even while the sun scorches the equator, water ice fills craters in the shadowed pole.

Mercury speeds around the sun once every 88 Earth days, but one day on Mercury is almost 176 Earth days long! Rotating three times on its axis for every two orbits around the sun, Mercury also has bizarre sunrises and sunsets. If you were standing on Mercury's equator, you would see the sun rise and set in different ways, depending on where you were. At some places, the sun would rise toward its high point in the sky, then stop and reverse direction, seeming to set. Then it would stop and rise again, getting smaller as it finally set in the west.

One day, as imagined here, astronauts may explore Mercury's Caloris Basin (art right), one of the largest craters in the solar system. Its diameter stretches 960 miles (1,550 km). It was created 400 million years ago, when a giant asteroid, with the impact of a trillion hydrogen bombs, slammed into the planet.

FACTS ABOUT MERCURY	
AVERAGE DISTANCE FROM THE SUN	35,983,125 MILES (57,909,227 KM)
POSITION FROM THE SUN IN ORBIT	FIRST
EQUATORIAL DIAMETER	3,030 MILES (4,878 KM)
MASS (EARTH = 1)	0.055
DENSITY (WATER = 1)	5.43
LENGTH OF DAY	176 EARTH DAYS
LENGTH OF YEAR	88 EARTH DAYS
SURFACE TEMPERATURES	-279°F (-173°C) TO 800°F (427°C)
KNOWN MOONS	0

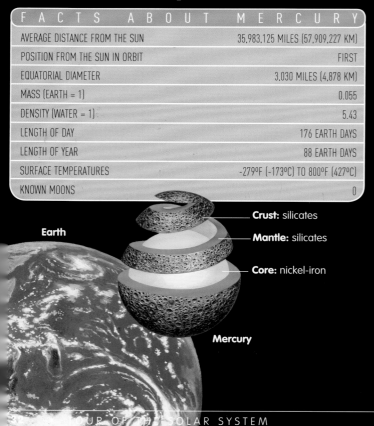

Earth

Crust: silicates

Mantle: silicates

Core: nickel-iron

Mercury

THE SUN

The sun is a middle-age star, about 4.6 billion years old. As the anchor that holds our solar system together, it provides the energy necessary for life to flourish on Earth. It accounts for 99 percent of the matter in the solar system. The rest of the planets, moons, asteroids, and comets added together amount to the remaining one percent.

Even though a million Earths could fit inside it, the sun is still considered an average-size star. Betelgeuse (say BET-el-jooz), the star on the shoulder of Orion in that constellation, is almost 400 times larger. Like other stars, the sun is a giant ball of hydrogen gas radiating heat and light through the process of

SHIP LOG DAY 2: Flyby of sun, use gravitational assist to accelerate

nuclear fusion. Unlike nuclear fission, in which atoms are split apart and create deadly radiation, fusion rams atoms together, producing cleaner and hotter reactions. Through fusion, the sun converts about four million tons of matter to energy every second.

Also like other stars, the sun revolves around its galaxy. Located halfway out in one of the arms of our Milky Way galaxy, the sun takes 225 to 250 million years to complete one revolution around the galaxy.

F A C T S A B O U T T H E S U N	
DIAMETER	870,000 MILES (1,390,000 KM)
AVERAGE TEMPERATURE	10,000°F (5500°C)
KIND OF STAR	YELLOW G2
AGE	4.6 BILLION YEARS

As our ship passes within a safe distance of the sun, a giant solar flare erupts (art right). Traveling away from us millions of miles across space (art left), a solar flare unleashes more energy than all the atomic bombs ever exploded on Earth combined.

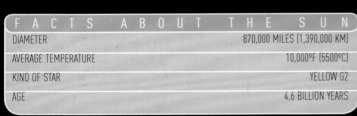

Earth

Sun

The sun is composed of about 92.1 percent hydrogen, 7.8 percent helium, and 0.1 percent trace elements like iron, carbon, lead, and uranium. These trace elements provide us with an amazing insight into the history of our star. They're the heavier elements that are produced when stars explode. Since these elements are relatively abundant in the sun, scientists know they were forged from the materials that came together in two previous star explosions. The sun and all the elements that are found in it and on Earth and in our bodies were recycled from those two exploding stars.

When viewed in space by astronauts, our sun burns white in color. When we see it from Earth, through our atmosphere, it looks like a yellow star. When astronomers study the sun's

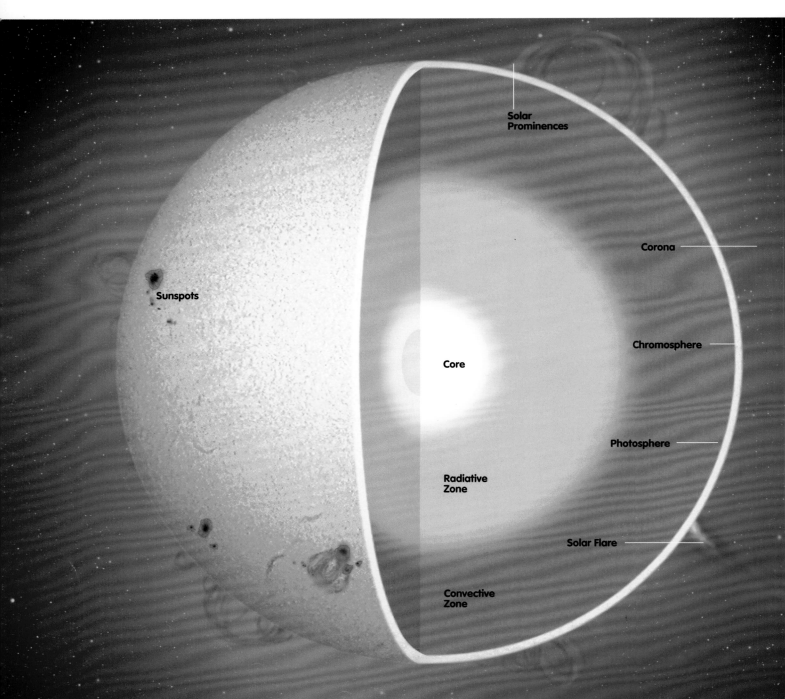

Solar Prominences

Corona

Sunspots

Chromosphere

Core

Photosphere

Radiative Zone

Solar Flare

Convective Zone

surface features, they see a much more complex structure than just a big, bright ball of gas. Most obvious are the sunspots. These blotches are slightly cooler areas that appear darker against the hotter background. The surface of the sun averages about 10,000°F (5500°C); the sunspots average about 6000°F (3316°C). Out of these sunspots shoot loops, or prominences, of superhot gas. These prominences follow invisible magnetic lines that connect the sunspots together. The loops extend for hundreds of miles above the photosphere, or visible surface of the sun. Solar flares, explosions of charged particles, sometimes erupt from the sun's surface into the farthest reaches of space. They create beautiful aurora displays on Earth, Jupiter, Saturn, and even on distant Uranus and Neptune.

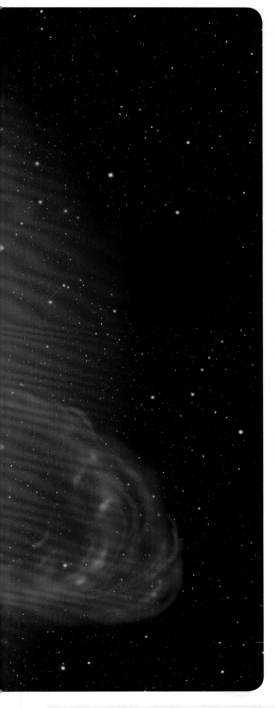

Above the sun's visible surface, or photosphere, is the chromosphere (art left)—a layer about a thousand miles (1,609 km) thick. Surrounding this is the corona, or crown. Scientists have discovered that the sun's corona is thousands of times hotter than its surface because the corona is heated by magnetic plasma.

In the satellite photograph above, the wispy streamers of gas in the sun's corona are visible, extending millions of miles into space. On Earth, the corona is only visible during a total eclipse of the sun.

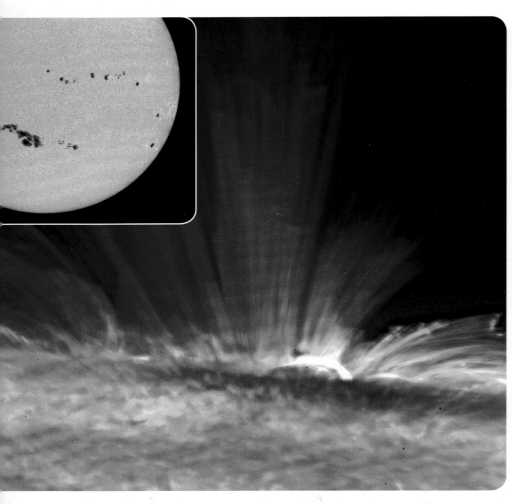

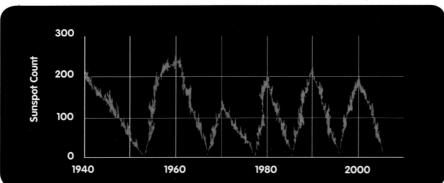

The sun has a huge magnetic field that reverses direction every 11 years (graph above). Sunspots, slightly cooler areas on the photosphere (photo top left), respond to these cycle changes. The largest ones are almost twice the size of Earth. Their frequency varies on an 11-year cycle, too.

The photo at the top right shows a solar flare erupting near the edge of the sun.

We know the sun makes life possible here on Earth. We couldn't survive without it. But it causes problems, too.

On October 28, 2003, we found out just how serious those problems can be. A huge solar flare shot highly charged energetic particles right at Earth, like bullets. Airplanes had to stop flying over the North and South Poles because passengers would have been exposed to increased radiation. A power blackout occurred in Sweden, and some satellites in orbit around the planet were

damaged. Many others, including the Hubble Space Telescope, had to be shut down and put into "safe" mode, to protect their delicate electronics.

As humans depend more and more on new technologies, they also face the prospect of overloaded power grids, a shutdown of electronic communications, and massive power blackouts caused by solar flares. Space travelers especially need to take extra precautions when one of these solar events occurs.

On dark winter nights, the northern sky (photo above) lights up with shimmering waves of green and red. Called aurora borealis, they are caused by charged particles in the solar winds colliding with atmospheric particles high above Earth.

MARS

Now we're coming to the planet nearest to Earth. Mars is about half the size of Earth, and it has some of the most spectacular scenery in the solar system. Its soaring canyons would stretch across North America, and its sky-scraping volcanoes overlook jumbled plains that may once have been shallow seas.

Mars also boasts polar ice caps, majestic sand dunes, impact craters formed millions of years ago, and dust devils that whirl around like small tornadoes. In the 19th century, astronomers began to think Martian engineers might have designed canals to crisscross the planet and bring water from the poles to Martian cities. That idea vanished when spacecraft reached Mars, but could it be capable of supporting microscopic life?

Liquid water is necessary for life on Earth. The atmosphere on Mars is so thin and the temperatures so cold that liquid water cannot exist on the surface. It would quickly freeze or evaporate. That's why there are no oceans. But there are signs that underground water does occasionally flow up to the surface. Mars might well have hidden wet habitats that are capable of supporting life.

SHIP LOG DAY 3: Approaching Mars, landing on its moon Phobos

FACTS ABOUT MARS	
AVERAGE DISTANCE FROM THE SUN	141,637,725 MILES (227,943,824 KM)
POSITION FROM THE SUN IN ORBIT	FOURTH
EQUATORIAL DIAMETER	4,220 MILES (6,792 KM)
MASS (EARTH = 1)	0.107
DENSITY (WATER = 1)	3.93
LENGTH OF DAY	26 EARTH HOURS
LENGTH OF YEAR	1.88 EARTH YEARS
SURFACE TEMPERATURES	-125°F (-87°C) TO 23°F (-5°C)
KNOWN MOONS	2

Mars

Earth

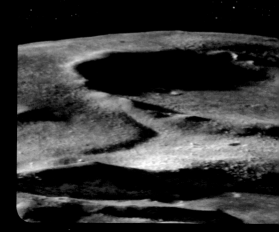

Mars looms like a great red sphere over the barren terrain of its largest moon, Phobos (art right), which orbits very close to the planet. Astronauts like those imagined here would have to be prepared for frigid nights.

An orange beacon in the night skies, Mars grows brighter and dimmer on a two-year cycle, as it moves closer to, then farther away from, Earth. It owes its distintive color to iron oxide in the soil. Like a piece of metal left outside, Mars has rusted. Although there are no thunderstorms here, weather is extremely unpredictable. Out of nowhere, blinding dust storms can blow up and blanket the landscape for months. Temperature swings are also enormous. Noontime highs can reach 70°F (20°C) around the equator, then at night dip to –100°F (–73°C). Mars's two

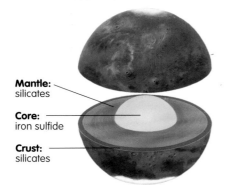

Mantle: silicates

Core: iron sulfide

Crust: silicates

Mars's rocky interior (art above) doesn't contain much metal, so the planet has only a tenth the mass of Earth and weak surface gravity, about a third of what we experience on Earth.

moons, Phobos and Deimos, appear to be captured asteroids. Unlike our moon, these two tiny space rocks zip across the night sky.

MISSIONS TO MARS

Dozens of spacecraft have flown by, orbited, or landed on Mars over the last 50 years or so. Recently, robotic rovers

Mars has the longest canyon in the solar system, the Valles Marinaris, seen as a dark slash around the planet's middle in the photo above. Measuring more than 3,100 miles (4,990 km) long, this huge system of valleys is some 120 miles (193 km) wide and 4 miles (6 km) deep. It was not carved by water but by the cooling and wrinkling of the landscape over time.

The photograph below was taken by the Mars Curiosity Rover. The rover landed on Mars in 2012 and sent back this image of a location on the Gale Crater called Point Lake. Curiosity has already discovered evidence that there may be dried streambeds on the planet.

have sent back pictures and scientific information directly from Mars's desertlike surface. NASA's Curiosity Rover, which landed on Mars in 2012, has been studying Martian soil. Scooping up sand with its robotic arm, it has found traces of an ancient streambed and—possibly—of molecules that may mean that Mars could once have hosted living organisms. Curiosity will keep looking for signs of life as it trundles along at about 98 feet (30 m) per hour.

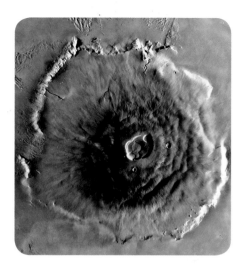

Mars has gigantic volcanoes on its surface that grow to a hundred times larger than they can on Earth. Soaring 14 miles (22 km) high, Olympus Mons (photo left) is the largest of four enormous volcanoes located near Mars's equator. Olympus Mons is a shield volcano, meaning it rises from the surface of the planet. The crater measures 53 miles (85 km) across, and the total area of the volcano is about the same as the state of New Mexico.

A close-up look at the Mars Curiosity Rover shows what this robot looks like in action. The size of a car, the rover was sent to Mars from Cape Canaveral, Florida, in November 2011 and landed on the planet in August 2012. As of March 2013, Curiosity was on the Gale Crater, with a move scheduled to Mt. Sharp to continue its exploration over the next few years.

CERES & THE ASTEROID BELT

Ceres is one of our newly named dwarf planets, a classification established in 2006. Astronomers have known about Ceres since 1801. When it was first discovered, they thought it might be the "missing planet" that many astronomers believed orbited between Mars and Jupiter. For the next half a century, it was called a planet. But then more and more large rocks, called asteroids, were discovered in that region of space. So Ceres was reclassified as an asteroid, and there it remained until its status changed to dwarf planet.

About 585 miles (940 km) in diameter, much smaller than our moon, Ceres is in the heart of

SHIP LOG DAY 4: Passing through asteroid belt, flyby of Ceres

the asteroid belt. Its mass is almost a third of the entire mass of the millions of asteroids in the belt.

Asteroids come in all shapes and sizes, but all of them orbit the sun. Collisions between them happen a lot, but these relics of the early solar system aren't crammed together as they're sometimes shown in science fiction movies.

Occasionally, the influence of Jupiter's gravity can nudge an asteroid out of orbit, sending it in toward the sun. When that happens, the asteroid can strike one of the terrestrial planets.

FACTS ABOUT CERES	
AVERAGE DISTANCE FROM THE SUN	257,055,204 MILES (413,690,250 KM)
POSITION FROM THE SUN IN ORBIT	FIFTH
EQUATORIAL DIAMETER	585 MILES (940 KM)
MASS (EARTH = 1)	0.00016
DENSITY (WATER = 1)	2.08
LENGTH OF DAY	9 EARTH HOURS
LENGTH OF YEAR	4.60 EARTH YEARS
AVERAGE SURFACE TEMPERATURE	-159°F (-106°C)
KNOWN MOONS	0

Ceres

Earth

Ceres (top right in artwork, right) lies deep inside the asteroid belt between the planets Mars and Jupiter, and is by far the largest object found here. Ceres and more than 200,000 other rocky objects called asteroids are the debris left over from the formation of the solar system.

JUPITER

Can you imagine a planet with no ground to walk on? Or a world where a red hurricane three times the size of Earth has been raging for centuries? What about a planet where ferocious winds rip through the skies at 400 miles (640 km) per hour, brilliant bolts of lightning blast across the sky, and auroras dance around the poles?

That planet, Jupiter, is coming up next on our tour. The largest planet in the solar system, Jupiter is so big that all the other planets, including Saturn, could easily fit inside it and still have room to spare. With at least 66 moons circling around it, Jupiter is almost a miniature solar system by itself.

No matter what instruments

SHIP LOG DAY 5: Approaching Jupiter, landing on its moon Europa

we use to view Jupiter, we can only see the tops of its clouds. In essence, we're looking at the outside of a gigantic slushy snowball.

Some people have called Jupiter a failed star. They say that if Jupiter had been just a little bit bigger when it formed, nuclear fires would have ignited deep inside it, radiating heat and light just like our sun. If that had happened, we would have had two suns in our sky instead of one.

FACTS ABOUT JUPITER	
AVERAGE DISTANCE FROM THE SUN	483,638,564 MILES (778,340,821 KM)
POSITION FROM THE SUN IN ORBIT	SIXTH
EQUATORIAL DIAMETER	86,880 MILES (139,800 KM)
MASS (EARTH = 1)	318
DENSITY (WATER = 1)	1.3
LENGTH OF DAY	9.9 EARTH HOURS
LENGTH OF YEAR	11.9 EARTH YEARS
AVERAGE SURFACE TEMPERATURE	-234ºF (-148ºC)
KNOWN MOONS	AT LEAST 66

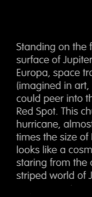

Jupiter

Earth

Standing on the frozen surface of Jupiter's moon Europa, space travelers (imagined in art, right) could peer into the Great Red Spot. This churning hurricane, almost three times the size of Earth, looks like a cosmic eye staring from the candy-striped world of Jupiter.

Days are very short on Jupiter. It spins so quickly on its axis that it makes one complete rotation every 9.9 Earth hours. Because it rotates so fast, it is not perfectly round. Egg-shaped, it bulges out around its equator like a spinning water balloon.

Composed of 90 percent hydrogen and almost 10 percent helium, its atmosphere would be poisonous for us to breathe. Here, little has changed since the planet formed 4.6 billion years ago.

Looking at Jupiter through a small telescope, we can easily see the two main features—the colored bands of clouds and the Great Red Spot. The white

The Great Red Spot (art below) is at least 350 years old, maybe older. Cyclonic storms like this are common on the gas giant planets and appear in a variety of colors. As we fly toward the Great Red Spot, we can see the moons Io (foreground) and Callisto (background).

Because of Jupiter's rapid rotation and solid metallic core, it generates the strongest planetary magnetic field in the solar system. The magnetic field, in turn, causes magnificent auroral displays that illuminate the northern and southern poles (art above).

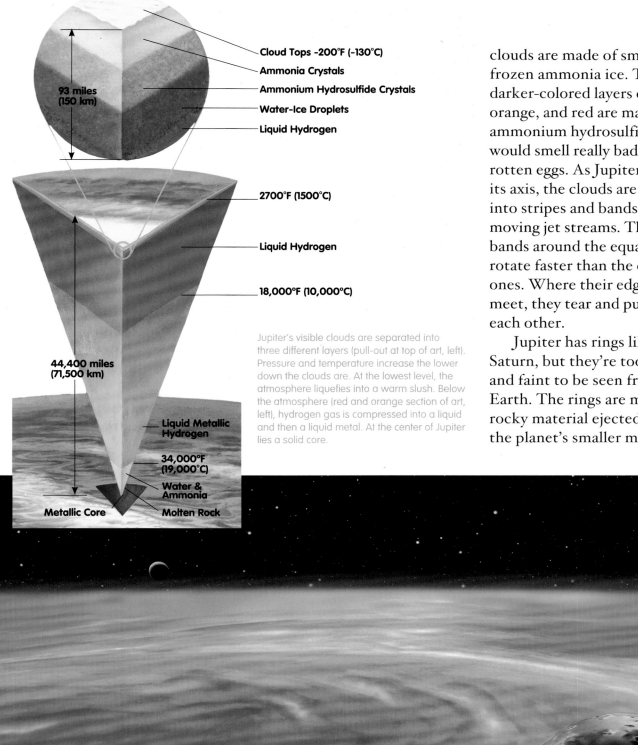

Cloud Tops -200°F (-130°C)
Ammonia Crystals
Ammonium Hydrosulfide Crystals
Water-Ice Droplets
Liquid Hydrogen

93 miles
(150 km)

2700°F (1500°C)

Liquid Hydrogen

18,000°F (10,000°C)

44,400 miles
(71,500 km)

Liquid Metallic
Hydrogen

34,000°F
(19,000°C)

Water &
Ammonia

Metallic Core

Molten Rock

Jupiter's visible clouds are separated into three different layers (pull-out at top of art, left). Pressure and temperature increase the lower down the clouds are. At the lowest level, the atmosphere liquefies into a warm slush. Below the atmosphere (red and orange section of art, left), hydrogen gas is compressed into a liquid and then a liquid metal. At the center of Jupiter lies a solid core.

clouds are made of smelly frozen ammonia ice. The darker-colored layers of brown, orange, and red are made of ammonium hydrosulfide. They would smell really bad, too, like rotten eggs. As Jupiter spins on its axis, the clouds are pulled into stripes and bands by fast-moving jet streams. The white bands around the equator rotate faster than the darker ones. Where their edges meet, they tear and pull at each other.

Jupiter has rings like Saturn, but they're too thin and faint to be seen from Earth. The rings are made of rocky material ejected from the planet's smaller moons.

Jupiter has at least 66 moons. The four largest can be seen through a pair of binoculars. They're called the Galilean moons because they were discovered by Galileo in 1610.

The first Galilean moon, Io, is located closest to Jupiter.

Almost the size of our moon, it's the most geologically active body in the solar system. Jupiter's gravitational pull bends and stretches Io like taffy, causing intense heating inside the moon. That causes volcanoes to erupt constantly on its surface.

Callisto is one of the most heavily cratered moons in the solar system. Its icy surface may be covering a salty ocean. If that ocean is liquid, Callisto would be a candidate for life in our solar system, but scientists suspect it is frozen solid.

ORBITS OF GALILEAN MOONS

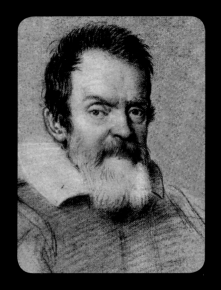

When Renaissance astronomer Galileo (art left) discovered Jupiter's moons Io, Europa, Ganymede, and Callisto in 1610, he called the four together the Medicean stars, in honor of his patron, Cosimo II de Medici, the Grand Duke of Tuscany. Galileo was hoping that, by conferring this honor on his patron, the grand duke would give him more money, so that his future research could be funded in style.

Galileo gave each moon a number instead of a name. But as more and more moons were discovered, the numbering system became a cumbersome way to refer to them. Finally, in the mid-1800s, the numbers were dropped, and the four Galilean moons were named after the girlfriends of the Greek god Zeus (Jupiter to the Romans).

All four Galilean moons (art below) are easily spotted with a pair of binoculars because they form a straight line on either side of Jupiter. Io is the closest, Europa, the second.

Ganymede, the third, is the largest moon in the entire solar system. Callisto, the last of the four, is one of the most heavily cratered moons in the solar system.

If you have a pair of binoculars or a small telescope, go out on a clear night and look for the Galilean moons.

Comparative Sizes

Europa Earth's Moon Io Callisto Ganymede

Jupiter Io Europa Ganymede Callisto

The surface of Io (photos above and right) looks like a pizza. The colors are layers of sulfur and lava that are constantly being sprayed out from very active volcanoes, like the one in the photograph on the right.

The heavily cratered surface of Callisto (photos above and right) was formed a long time ago—maybe four billion years in the past. Unlike Europa, Callisto seems to be frozen solid, with no liquid oceans hidden under its surface of thick ice.

Ganymede (photos below and left) is bigger than our moon and the planet Mercury, as well as dwarf planets Pluto, Eris, and Ceres.

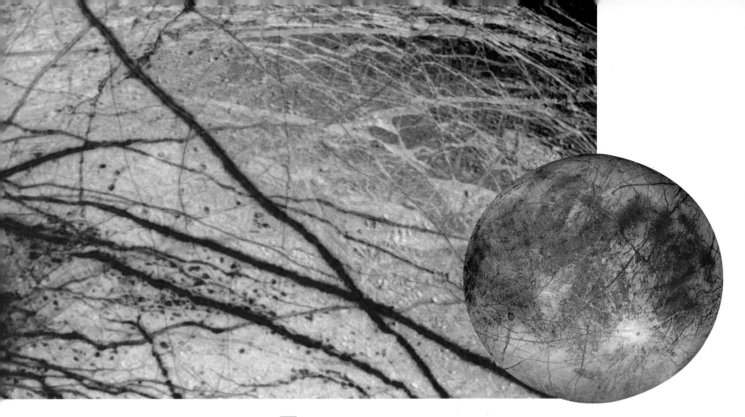

The Galilean moon Ganymede is the largest moon in the solar system. If it circled the sun, it would be considered a planet and would be the eighth largest in the solar system.

The darker regions of Ganymede are its original icy surfaces that have been covered with meteorites and dust. This Jovian moon appears to be frozen solid, but it could have liquid oceans under the ice. Astronomers don't know yet.

Europa is slightly smaller than Io. It has an icy surface that covers a hidden saltwater ocean. Water was important for life to begin here on Earth, and Europa may have even more water than Earth. This means that Europa is an excellent place to look for life in the solar system. But drilling through the 16 miles (26 km) of solid ice that covers these oceans will be a real challenge.

When Galileo discovered these moons, most people still believed that Earth was the center of the solar system. They thought that all the heavenly bodies revolved around Earth. These four moons of Jupiter provided the first real evidence that there was something in outer space that did not rotate around Earth.

The face of Europa (photos above and left) is deceptive. Its icy surface looks like a mosaic of giant cracks. However, there is much more to this moon than meets the eye. Underneath all the ice is a saltwater ocean that may be more than 60 miles (97 km) deep.

Monitoring a drilling rig, future astronauts (imagined in art, left) bore down through the 16 miles (26 km) of ice covering the surface of Europa. The challenge is keeping the freshly drilled hole from immediately freezing over, so that a robotic probe can be inserted through the hole to explore the mysterious dark waters below.

SATURN

When people first see Saturn through a telescope, they usually gasp in wonder. As our spaceship gets close to the seventh planet, we can see its beauty close up. No other planet in the solar system has the visual splendor of Saturn.

When Galileo pointed his own crude telescope toward it in 1610, the telescope was not good enough to separate the rings from the rest of the disk. So he thought he'd found a "triple-bodied" planet.

Today, we know all four gas giant planets have rings, but Saturn's are the only ones visible by telescope from Earth. Surrounded by a brilliant halo of ice and dust, Saturn seems to

SHIP LOG DAY 8: Approaching Saturn, orbiting its moon Mimas

mimic the formation of the early solar system. The diameters of its rings together span some 175,000 miles (282,000 km), about three-quarters of the distance from our moon to Earth. Traveling at the speed of a jet, it would take ten days and nights to cross Saturn's rings. As amazing as this is, even more astounding is the fact that some rings have areas that are more than 2 miles (3 km) thick.

FACTS ABOUT SATURN	
AVERAGE DISTANCE FROM THE SUN	886,489,415 MILES (1,426,666,422 KM)
POSITION FROM THE SUN IN ORBIT	SEVENTH
EQUATORIAL DIAMETER	72,370 MILES (116,460 KM)
MASS (EARTH = 1)	95
DENSITY (WATER = 1)	0.69
LENGTH OF DAY	10 EARTH HOURS
LENGTH OF YEAR	30 EARTH YEARS
AVERAGE SURFACE TEMPERATURE	-288°F (-178°C)
KNOWN MOONS	AT LEAST 62

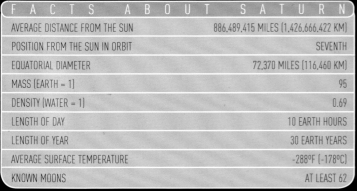

Earth

Saturn

Liquid Hydrogen

Liquid Metallic Hydrogen

Water & Ammonia

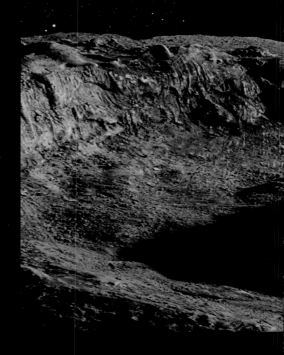

If you were standing in the giant Herschel Crater on Saturn's moon Mimas (art right), the planet would fill the sky. From this viewpoint, it's easy to see how thin the planet's rings actually are.

Like Jupiter, Saturn has no surface to walk on. Its slushy atmosphere is mostly liquid hydrogen and helium, driven by gale-force winds into pale, colored bands and stripes. Occasionally, large white, oval-shaped storms appear, similar to the Great Red Spot on Jupiter.

Saturn spins very quickly on its axis, completing a rotation every 10 hours 14 minutes. But it takes 30 years to make one orbit around the sun. Its magnetic field is about 600 times stronger than Earth's, producing aurora fireworks that change hourly.

Saturn's rings reflect back 70 percent of the light from the sun and are sometimes even brighter than the planet. Ring names are assigned letters alphabetically in order of their discovery. Right now, they have names that go from A through G. The rings may have formed within the past 50 to 100 million years, either from the breakup of an icy moon or a captured asteroid. Astronomers think the object would have been about 240 miles (386 km) in diameter.

The particles from this captured body are still gravitationally attracted to one another, as if the body were trying to reassemble itself.

The rings consist of thousands of closely spaced bands, called ringlets, with gaps in between them. The largest gap, the Cassini Division, is about 3,000 miles (4,700 km) wide and visible from Earth through a telescope. The rings change over time, and every 15 years, when they face Earth edge-on, they disappear from our view. Early astronomers questioned their own reasoning when they noticed that the rings vanished, only to reappear a few years later. The next time the rings disappear will be in 2023.

This remarkable photograph of Saturn was taken by the Cassini spacecraft as it passed along the shadowed back side of the ringed planet. From this angle, with the sun hidden, a wonder never before seen came into view— the E ring, the faint one farthest out in the photograph. It is invisible to telescopes on Earth.

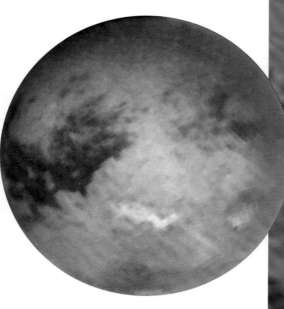

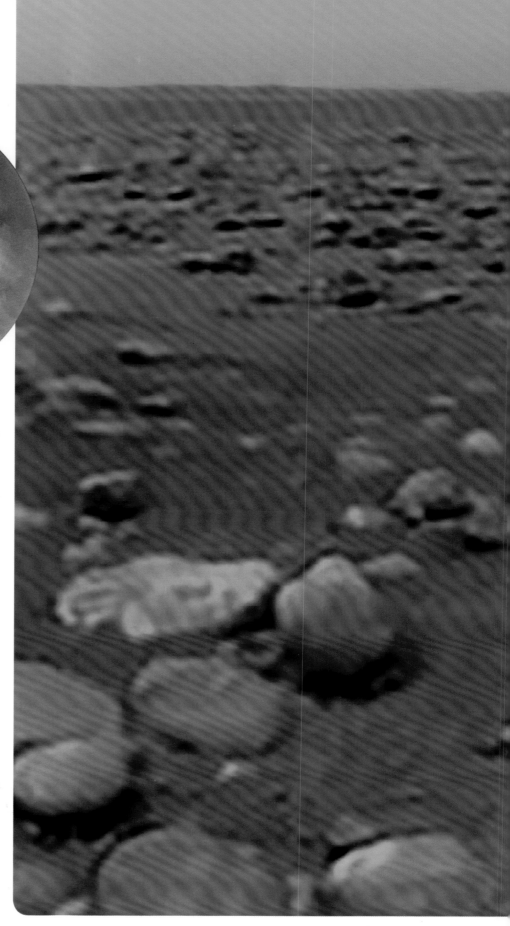

The largest and most intriguing of Saturn's moons, Titan (photo above) is nearly half the size of Earth. A photograph (right), taken by the Huygens spacecraft, shows Titan cloaked in a thick orange atmospheric haze; the small rocks in the foreground are only a few inches in size.

Like Jupiter, Saturn has a fascinating array of moons—at least 62 of them. The precise number is uncertain, and most are quite small and oddly shaped. Still, seven are massive enough to have formed into spheres under the influence of their own gravity.

Titan, the second largest moon in the solar system after Jupiter's Ganymede, is bigger in diameter than Mercury and any of the known dwarf planets. It's the only moon in the solar system with a substantial atmosphere. Underneath Titan's dense orange blanket of clouds is a primordial world brimming with mysteries. Because the

atmosphere is so thick and the gravity so low, humans could fly through it by attaching wings to their arms and flapping them up and down like butterflies. The moon's surface holds dark lakes of liquid methane with drainage channels rimming the shore-lines. Scientists believe the early atmosphere on Earth was very similar to the atmosphere on Titan today. If that is so, Titan is one of the objects in the solar system, along with Earth, Mars, Jupiter's Europa, and possibly Saturn's Enceladus, that may harbor life.

Mimas, about 240 miles (385 km) in diameter, is composed mostly of frozen ice and some rock. It sports one of the biggest black eyes in the solar system—a crater that is almost 80 miles (130 km) in diameter. The crater is named Herschel for Sir William Herschel, who discovered Mimas in 1789.

The huge crater on Mimas (photo above) was caused by a collision with a giant piece of space debris that almost destroyed the moon sometime in the distant past.

Dione's surface markings (photo above) resemble the dark marks on our moon and were probably caused by water flooding the surface and quickly freezing.

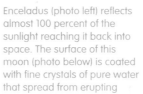

Enceladus (photo left) reflects almost 100 percent of the sunlight reaching it back into space. The surface of this moon (photo below) is coated with fine crystals of pure water that spread from erupting water volcanoes.

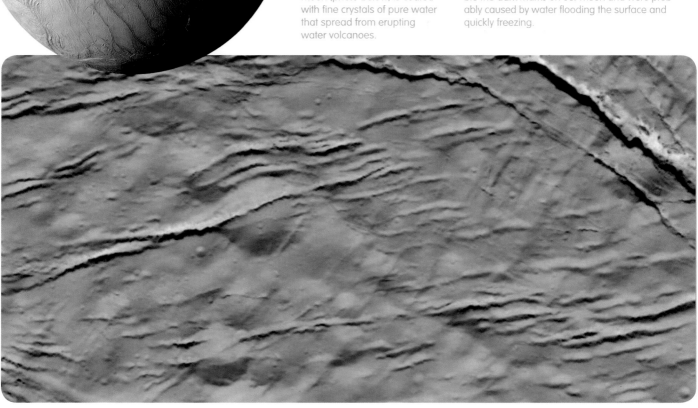

U R A N U S

As we approach Uranus, it glows like an aquamarine gem in the outer reaches of our solar system.

Like Neptune, this planet is an icy giant. Neither has a solid surface. Uranus's blue-green color is caused by the absorption of red wavelengths of distant sunlight entering its frosty atmosphere. Methane gas reflects the blue and green wavelengths back into space.

Unlike any other planet, Uranus has a 98-degree tilt to its axis. Hit by something gigantic long ago, it almost lies on its side! Right now, its north pole faces the sun, while the south pole faces away into space. This brings 42 years of constant

SHIP LOG DAY 11: Approaching Uranus, landing on its moon Miranda

sunlight to one side of the planet, followed by 42 years of complete darkness.

Since Uranus is tipped over on its side, its 13 thin, wispy rings do not circle it the way Saturn's rings do.

Of all the planets, Uranus may boast the greatest literary roots. Its 27 known moons are named mostly after characters from the works of William Shakespeare, the great English playwright. Two of its largest moons, Oberon and Titania, are named for the king and queen of the fairies.

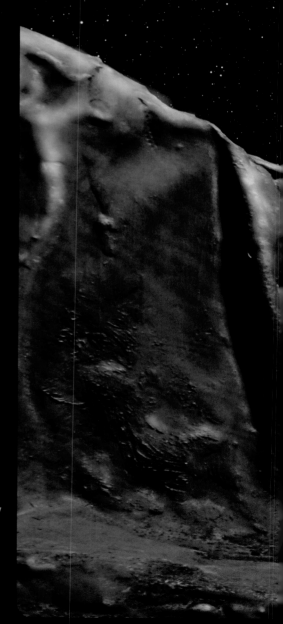

FACTS ABOUT URANUS	
AVERAGE DISTANCE FROM THE SUN	1,783,744,300 MILES (2,870,658,186 KM)
POSITION FROM THE SUN IN ORBIT	EIGHTH
EQUATORIAL DIAMETER	31,500 MILES (50,724 KM)
MASS (EARTH = 1)	15
DENSITY (WATER = 1)	1.27
LENGTH OF DAY	17.9 EARTH HOURS
LENGTH OF YEAR	84 EARTH YEARS
AVERAGE SURFACE TEMPERATURE	-357°F (-216°C)
KNOWN MOONS	27

Earth

Molten Rock

Water & Ammonia

Hydrogen & Helium

Uranus

Astronauts visiting Uranus's moon Miranda (imagined in art, right) would clearly see the way the planet spins tipped over on its axis. The surface of Miranda would probably be slippery to walk on because of the ice and snow that scientists think erupt from its water volcanoes.

NEPTUNE

We're nearing the pale blue, icy world of Neptune. It has the wildest weather of any planet in the solar system, with winds that blow at speeds over 1,200 miles (2,000 km) per hour.

Like the other Jovian planets, Neptune doesn't have a surface to walk on. Although the clouds surrounding it are very cold, -350°F (-212°C), its rocky iron core is about the same temperature as the sun's surface. This internal heat causes the planet's violent winds and hurricanes. Dark spots, or storms, similar to Jupiter's Great Red Spot dot its surface. The largest, called the Great Dark Spot, is no longer seen, but was bigger than

SHIP LOG DAY 17: Approaching Neptune, close flyby of its moon Triton

Earth. Astronomers call one of the lighter-colored spots Scooter because this small, fast-moving storm seems to chase other storms around. Six rings surround the planet.

Neptune was detected by mathematical calculation rather than observation in 1846. Astronomers realized something very large was affecting the orbit of Uranus. That something was Neptune, even though it lies a billion miles farther out in space.

Since its discovery more than 160 years ago, Neptune has completed only one full orbit of the sun!

FACTS ABOUT NEPTUNE	
AVERAGE DISTANCE FROM THE SUN	2,795,173,960 MILES (4,498,396,441 KM)
POSITION FROM THE SUN IN ORBIT	NINTH
EQUATORIAL DIAMETER	30,775 MILES (49,528 KM)
MASS (EARTH = 1)	17
DENSITY (WATER = 1)	1.64
LENGTH OF DAY	16 EARTH HOURS
LENGTH OF YEAR	164.8 EARTH YEARS
AVERAGE SURFACE TEMPERATURE	-353°F (-214°C)
KNOWN MOONS	13

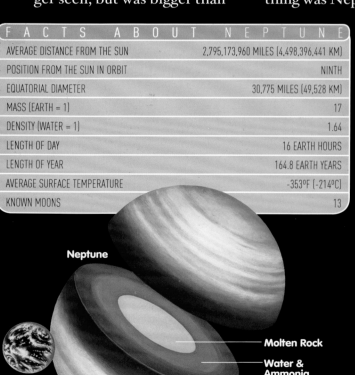

Neptune

Earth

Molten Rock

Water & Ammonia

Hydrogen & Helium

Neptune's blue methane clouds help illuminate the frozen surface of its large moon, Triton (art right). Astronauts here would have to be careful of the surface gashes, craters, and large frozen lakes caused by erupting water volcanoes.

K U I P E R   B E L T

A huge concentration of galactic debris and assorted planetary leftovers make up a faraway region known as the Kuiper (rhymes with *viper*) belt. It extends from the orbit of Neptune to hundreds of millions of miles beyond the dwarf planet Pluto.

Astronomers believe that after the gas giant planets had taken shape during the formation of the solar system, gravitational interactions between Jupiter and Saturn may have ejected this galactic debris far out into space.

Today, the dwarf planets Pluto, Haumea, Makemake, and Eris, as well as their moons, are all considered members of the Kuiper belt. So are Halley's comet and the other "short-period" comets that make regular trips around the sun every 200 years or more. So far, more than 1,300 KBOs (Kuiper belt objects) have been identified and numbered. But there may be more than 100,000 of these icy objects, each with the potential of becoming a new comet in Earth's nighttime skies.

Orbit of Neptune   **Kuiper Belt**

In the Kuiper belt, asteroids smash together, sometimes nudging each other into new orbits toward the sun. Here (art right), we see in the distance, they vaporize and grow large tails, becoming spectacular comets. Periodically returning comets, like Halley's comet, originate in the Kuiper belt.

PLUTO

For 76 years, Pluto reigned as the ninth planet in our solar system. In 2006, everything changed. Like a popular sports star who gets demoted to second string, Pluto has been reclassified as a dwarf planet.

Originally, astronomers thought Pluto might be about the size of Earth. Its true size was difficult to tell because it was so far away. No matter what telescope was used to look at it, no details could be seen. It simply appeared as a speck of light. The best the Hubble Space Telescope could do was capture an image of a small ball with patches of dark and light. We now know Pluto is smaller than our own moon.

SHIP LOG DAY 25: Approaching Pluto, sightseeing flyby

Pluto is located in the Kuiper belt, where comets that return again and again originate. Made of rock and ice, it's very cometlike in composition. If this dwarf planet could somehow be relocated near the sun, it would have a tail and look a lot like a comet.

Pluto also has a large moon named Charon (SHAR-on). Because of their sizes, Pluto and Charon together are considered a dwarf double-planet by many astronomers.

FACTS ABOUT PLUTO	
AVERAGE DISTANCE FROM THE SUN	3,670,092,055 MILES (5,906,440,628 KM)
POSITION FROM THE SUN IN ORBIT	TENTH
EQUATORIAL DIAMETER	1,485 MILES (2,400 KM)
MASS (EARTH = 1)	0.002
DENSITY (WATER = 1)	2.05
LENGTH OF DAY	6.39 EARTH DAYS
LENGTH OF YEAR	248 EARTH YEARS
AVERAGE SURFACE TEMPERATURE	-369°F (-220°C)
KNOWN MOONS	5

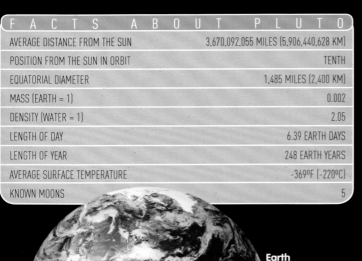

Earth

Pluto

The Milky Way stretches behind the dwarf planet Pluto and its large moon, Charon (art right). In the distance, two of Pluto's smaller moons, Nix and Hydra, can be seen silhouetted against the starlit sky. Pluto is known to have a total of five moons.

Pluto's story begins with the discovery of Neptune. Realizing there was something odd about the orbit of Uranus, early astronomers theorized there might be another planet pulling on it. After searching for many years, they discovered Neptune in 1846.

After that, observations of Neptune indicated something was disturbing its orbit, too. Was there another undiscovered planet out there? In 1905, Percival Lowell began searching for this Planet X from his observatory in Flagstaff, Arizona.

Today, we know that Pluto is too small to have had any influence on Neptune, but Lowell spent the rest of his life searching for the undiscovered planet. He never found it, but a night assistant at the Lowell Observatory named Clyde Tombaugh did.

At 22 years old, Tombaugh (photo right) built his own six-inch reflecting telescope and sent drawings of Mars and Jupiter to the Lowell Observatory. Scientists there offered him a job, and he began taking pictures of the same area of the sky a week apart. If an object changed position on one of the photographic plates, it might be Planet X. On February 18, 1930,

something showed up on one of Tombaugh's plates. Everyone was amazed. This object became the ninth planet in the solar system.

The right to name it belonged to the Lowell Observatory. The observatory scientists asked for name submissions, and an 11-year-old English girl came up with Pluto! Shortly after that, Disney Studios named Mickey Mouse's dog Pluto in honor of this new planet. Pluto's astronomical symbol, PL, stands for the first two letters in its name and honors the initials of Percival Lowell.

In 2006, everything changed. After three new planet-like objects about Pluto's size were discovered in the Kuiper belt, astronomers began wondering just how many more might be out there. At a meeting, the International Astronomical Union considered whether other dwarf planets should be upgraded to full planet status or whether Pluto should be downgraded. Debate among the astronomers turned into arguments that went

on for days, but in the end, Pluto was downgraded.

But Pluto's demotion created more problems. The new definition for a planet says it must be round, it must orbit the sun, and it must have cleared out smaller debris from its orbit. Pluto hasn't cleared out debris from its orbit, but neither have Earth, Mars, Jupiter, and Neptune. In other words, by this definition, they aren't planets, either.

The debate about Pluto is probably not over yet.

Pluto and Charon's very peculiar orbit around the sun is egg-shaped instead of circular. They orbit so far out on the edge of the solar system that from the surface of Pluto, the sun would look like just another bright star in the sky. Besides Charon, Pluto has four smaller moons named Nix, Hydra, P4, and P5.

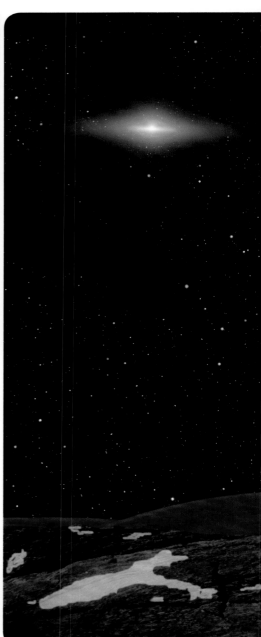

In a couple of years, we should know a lot more about the distant world of Pluto. On July 14, 2015, the New Horizons spacecraft will fly by Pluto, showing us this little world up close for the first time. New Horizons' trip is no small feat. The spacecraft will take nine years to reach the dwarf planet.

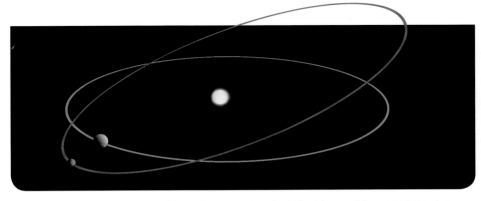

All the other planets, except Eris, orbit in a flat plane in nearly circular orbits, but Pluto's orbit (art above) is inclined 17 degrees above the plane in an elliptical (oval) instead of a circular orbit.

Pluto (art below) is one of the coldest objects in the solar system. In fact, when it is at its farthest from the sun, its atmosphere freezes, like a thin ice frosting on the ground.

H A U M E A

Leaving Pluto behind, we travel even farther into the lonely reaches of the Kuiper belt in search of the next two dwarf planets. Before long, we spot one of the oddest members of the solar system.

Tumbling end over end is potato-shaped Haumea, circled by two tiny moons. Thin ice covers its rocky surface. The dwarf planet, about as long as Pluto is wide, spins so quickly that it has just a four-hour day. But its year is long—Haumea takes 285 Earth years to orbit the sun.

Haumea has one of the fastest rotations of any large body in the solar system. Astronomers think a collision early in its history sent it

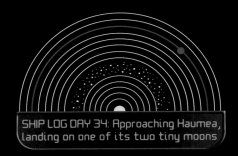

SHIP LOG DAY 34: Approaching Haumea, landing on one of its two tiny moons

whirling, and that this motion gradually pulled it into its oblong shape. The impact may also have knocked off the chunks of rock that make up its moons, Namaka and Hi'iaka. Astronomer Mike Brown, one of the spinning world's discoverers, nicknamed it "Santa" because he spotted it just after Christmas in 2004. Its official name, Haumea, comes from the Hawaiian goddess of fertility and childbirth. The moons are named after two of the goddess's daughters.

FACTS ABOUT HAUMEA	
AVERAGE DISTANCE FROM THE SUN	4,090,055,520 MILES (6,582,306,310 KM)
POSITION FROM THE SUN IN ORBIT	ELEVENTH
EQUATORIAL DIAMETER	808 MILES (1,300 KM)
MASS (EARTH = 1)	0.00066
DENSITY (WATER = 1)	3
LENGTH OF DAY	3.9 EARTH HOURS
LENGTH OF YEAR	285 EARTH YEARS
AVERAGE SURFACE TEMPERATURE	-396°F (-233°C)
KNOWN MOONS	2

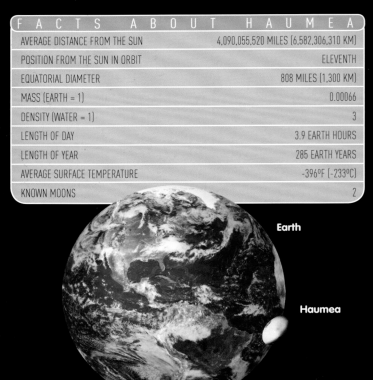

Earth

Haumea

Shaped like an egg, Haumea (art right) is one of the oldest known objects in the solar system. It's as big across as Pluto, and every four hours it spins end over end, like a kicked football. Mostly rock, this dwarf planet appears to have an icy covering that makes it shine as it travels through space.

M A K E M A K E

Dwarf planet Makemake is next on our tour of the solar system's chilly fringe. It shows up ahead of us, bright and surprisingly red. Unlike Haumea, Makemake has a normal round shape, though a bit flattened at the poles. It is somewhat smaller than Pluto. (Because it doesn't have moons, which help astronomers measure mass, we aren't quite sure how massive it is.) Just one orbit around the sun takes 310 years.

Makemake is thickly covered with ice—not water ice, but ice made of ethane, methane, and nitrogen. If sound could travel on its airless surface, you might hear the ice grains crunch under your feet. Radiation from the sun has turned the ice a reddish-brown color. It is cold cold cold down there—about -406°F (-240°C).

Makemake was originally nicknamed Easterbunny, because it was discovered just after Easter in 2005. Its official name comes from Easter Island. Makemake is a chief god in the mythology of the Rapanui people.

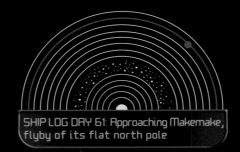

SHIP LOG DAY 61: Approaching Makemake, flyby of its flat north pole

FACTS ABOUT MAKEMAKE

AVERAGE DISTANCE FROM THE SUN	4,275,967,134 MILES (6,881,502,052 KM)
POSITION FROM THE SUN IN ORBIT	TWELFTH
EQUATORIAL DIAMETER	889 MILES (1,430 KM)
MASS (EARTH = 1)	0.0005
DENSITY (WATER = 1)	1.70
LENGTH OF DAY	3.8 EARTH HOURS
LENGTH OF YEAR	310 EARTH YEARS
AVERAGE SURFACE TEMPERATURE	-398°F (-239°C)
KNOWN MOONS	0

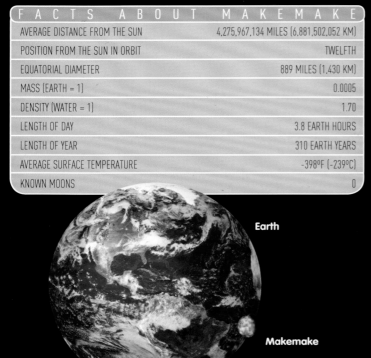

Earth

Makemake

The odd, red-colored dwarf planet Makemake reflects just enough dim sunlight to be seen in large telescopes back on Earth. To the right, the stunning open star cluster, the Pleiades, shines like blue sapphire jewels.

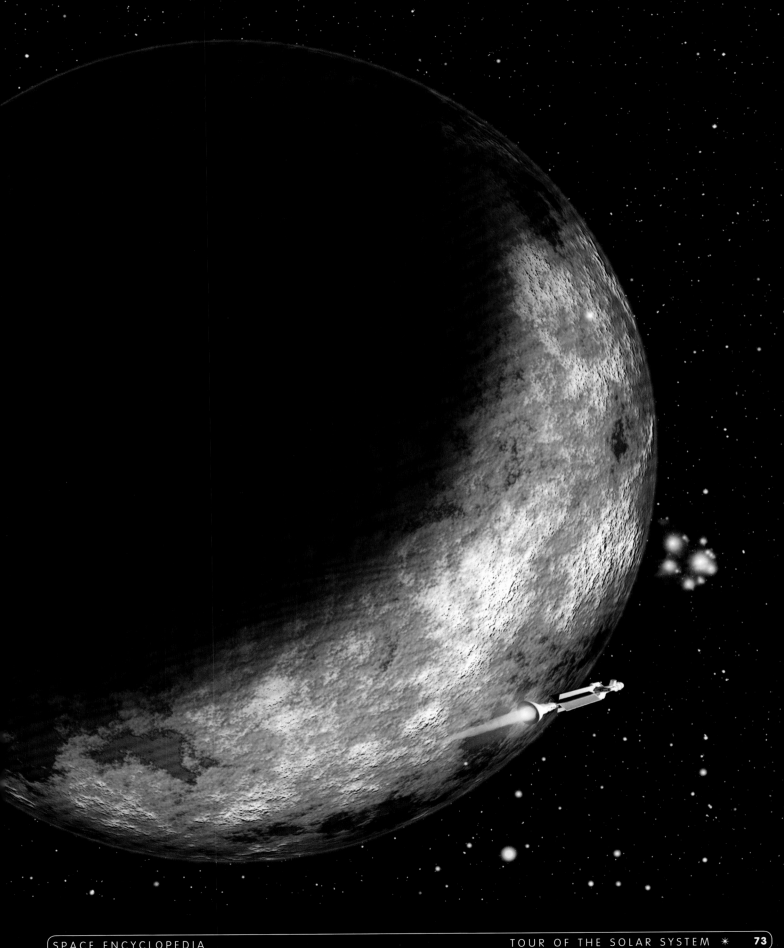

ERIS

The coldest object ever found in our solar system is now looming before us. Eris was discovered in 2005. It has an orbit that goes through the Kuiper belt but also extends beyond it—nine billion miles (14 billion km) from the sun. Eris orbits the sun about every 560 Earth years! It's about the same size as Pluto and has a moon named Dysnomia.

Eris's discoverer, Mike Brown, was amazed to find something so far out in the solar system. When it became classified as a new planet, some astronomers weren't too happy. If Pluto remained a planet, and Ceres and Eris were added to the list too, the solar system might keep expanding until we

SHIP LOG DAY 84: Approaching Eris, initiate return journey to Earth!

had more planets than anyone could name. Instead, at the 2006 meeting of the International Astronomical Union, scientists came up with the new classification of dwarf planet, which included Pluto.

Pluto, Ceres, Haumea, Makemake, and Eris are different from the other eight planets. They're smaller than some of the moons of Jupiter, they're a combination of rock and ice, and their orbits are different from the others.

Right now, our solar system has 13 planets. But there are probably more out in space we haven't discovered yet.

FACTS ABOUT ERIS

AVERAGE DISTANCE FROM THE SUN	6,325,635,074 MILES (10,180,122,852 KM)
POSITION FROM THE SUN IN ORBIT	THIRTEENTH
EQUATORIAL DIAMETER	1,678 MILES (2,700 KM)
MASS (EARTH = 1)	0.0028
DENSITY (WATER = 1)	2.1
LENGTH OF DAY	1.1 EARTH DAYS
LENGTH OF YEAR	561 EARTH YEARS
AVERAGE SURFACE TEMPERATURE	-406°F (-243°C)
KNOWN MOONS	1

Earth

Eris

The new dwarf planet Eris and its moon, Dysnomia (art right), are as far as our expedition through the solar system takes us. This icy distant rock is the largest of the new dwarf planets and the most distant from the sun.

OORT CLOUD

If we could travel 465 trillion miles (748 trillion km) from the sun, out past the extreme edges of the solar system, astronomers think that we would encounter an enormous cloud known as the Oort cloud. They also think this is the remains of the original nebula that coalesced to form our solar system nearly 4.6 billion years ago. The cloud marks the outer boundaries of the sun's gravitational field.

In 1950, Dutch astronomer Jan Oort set out to determine the origin of comets. He proposed that a vast and remote reservoir existed one to two light-years from the sun, far beyond Pluto's orbit. Although no one has actually observed the Oort cloud, astronomers believe it's the base camp for most comets. These icy fragments probably orbit the sun here until a passing star's gravity nudges one of them, sending it on a new journey in toward the sun. Since comets zoom in from all directions, astronomers think the Oort cloud wraps around the solar system.

Other stars may also have Oort-like clouds around them. The icy comets in these clouds could help future space travelers on their way. Water ice from the comets could provide hydrogen to power their ships, water to drink, and oxygen to breathe.

Though the Oort cloud (art left) has not yet been detected by astronomical instruments, scientists believe that not only our solar system but other star systems as well may have Oort clouds. The art at right shows a cloud around our solar system (middle), Alpha Centauri (lower right), and other, more distant stars.

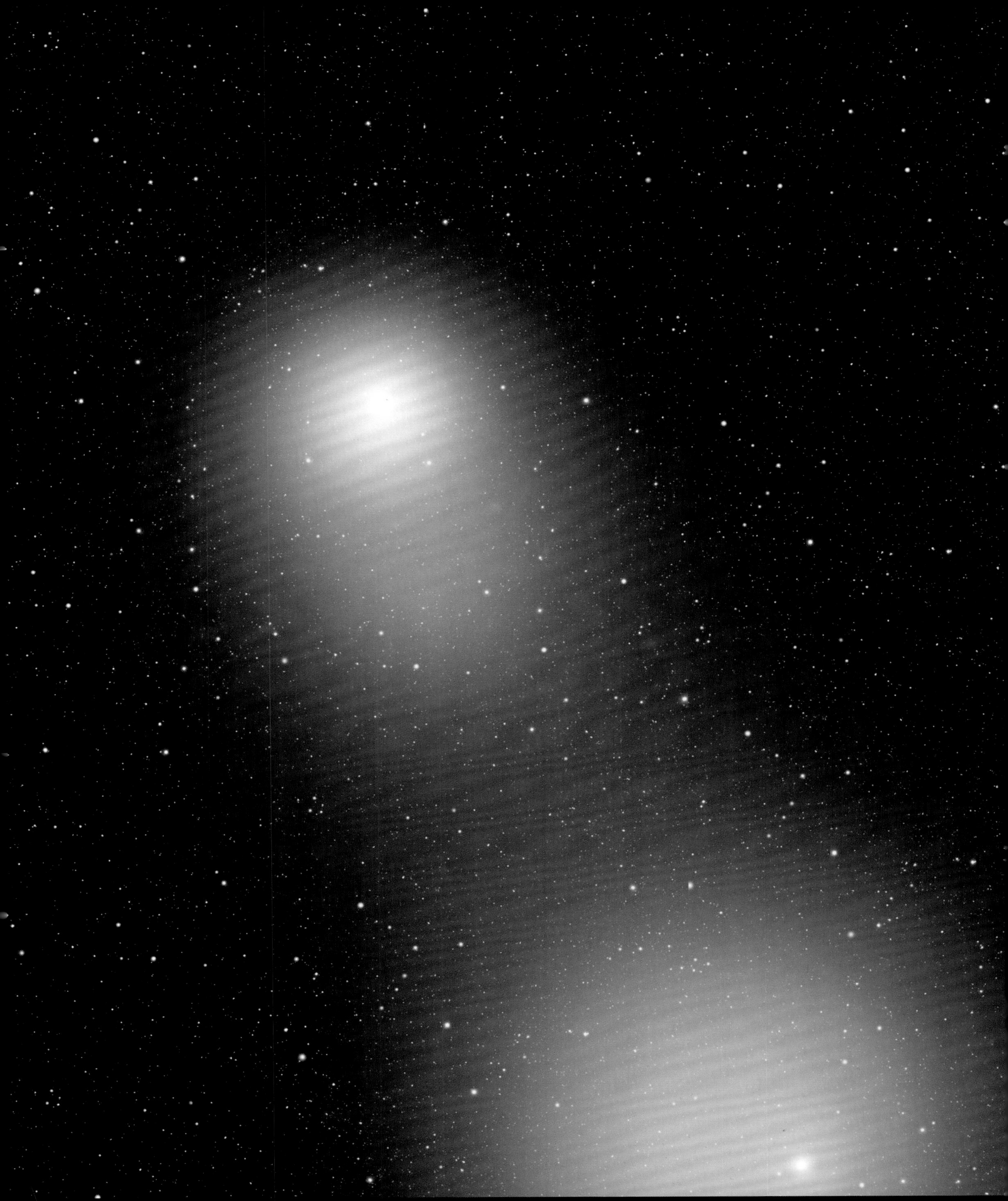

COMETS

Of all the objects in the night sky, comets are the most spectacular. Most of these unexpected visitors originate far out in the Oort cloud, where they take hundreds, even millions, of years to complete one orbit around the sun. A second major group comes from the Kuiper belt. They're called short-period comets because their orbital periods are less than 200 years. Halley's comet, one of the most famous short-period comets of all time, comes from this area.

The word comet comes from the Greek word *kometes,* which means "long-haired."

Today, we know that these objects are leftovers from the formation of the solar system 4.6 billion years ago. Made of sand, water ice, and carbon dioxide, comets have been called big, dirty snowballs.

As they pass by Jupiter on their way toward the sun, comets begin to defrost. Solar heating vaporizes ice, which forms a halo of gas and dust, or coma, around the comet's nucleus. As they near the orbit of Mars, they may start to form long spectacular tails, sometimes hundreds of millions of miles long. Blown by the solar wind, the tails of comets always point away from the sun.

Parts of a Comet

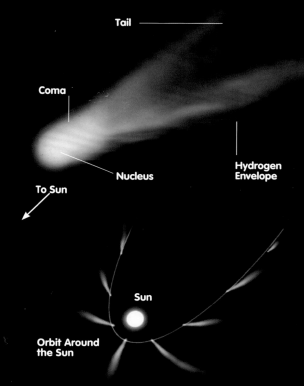

Tail

Coma

Nucleus

Hydrogen
Envelope

To Sun

Sun

Orbit Around
the Sun

Low in the west, just after sunset, the tail of a brilliant comet lights up the evening sky (art right). Short-period comets, such as Halley's comet, return every 200 years or sooner in their journeys around the sun. The comet pictured here is a long-period comet that will not return again for thousands of years.

EARTH

Our tour of the solar system is coming to an end, and we're heading home. Now that we've visited other planets, we can appreciate more than ever what a Garden of Eden our Earth is.

From space, Earth appears deep blue because of the nitrogen in the atmosphere and the oceans that cover 71 percent of its surface. Since Earth spins on its axis more than 1,000 miles (1,600 km) per hour and travels around the sun at 66,700 miles (107,300 km) per hour, all of us who live on Earth are actually traveling through space all the time!

Located at just the right distance from the sun, Earth is warm enough for water to exist

SHIP LOG DAY 199: Back to Earth. It's a long, strange trip back home.

as a liquid, which is an essential element for most life. Its atmosphere is oxygen-rich and swirled by white clouds. And Earth has the most diverse terrain of any planet. The polar caps are covered with sheets of ice. Along the Equator, vast deserts border grasslands that give way to lush tropical jungles. In temperate zones, green forests surround mountains thrust up by volcanoes or the movements of tectonic plates.

So far, our planet is the only place in the universe we know of that has life on it.

FACTS ABOUT EARTH	
AVERAGE DISTANCE FROM THE SUN	92,956,050 MILES (149,598,262 KM)
POSITION FROM THE SUN IN ORBIT	THIRD
EQUATORIAL DIAMETER	7,900 MILES (12,750 KM)
MASS (EARTH = 1)	1
DENSITY (WATER = 1)	5.51
LENGTH OF DAY	24 HOURS
LENGTH OF YEAR	365 DAYS
SURFACE TEMPERATURES	-126°F (-88°C) TO 136°F (58°C)
KNOWN MOONS	1

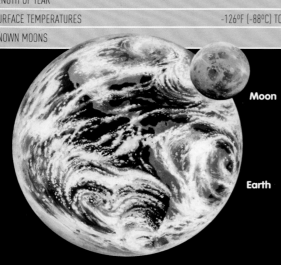

Moon

Earth

Earth (art right) is the crown jewel of our solar system, at least from a human perspective. Returning to this blue world, we can see that it is daytime in India (center), the Middle East (slightly to the left), and Africa (far left). On the opposite side of the world, it's nighttime.

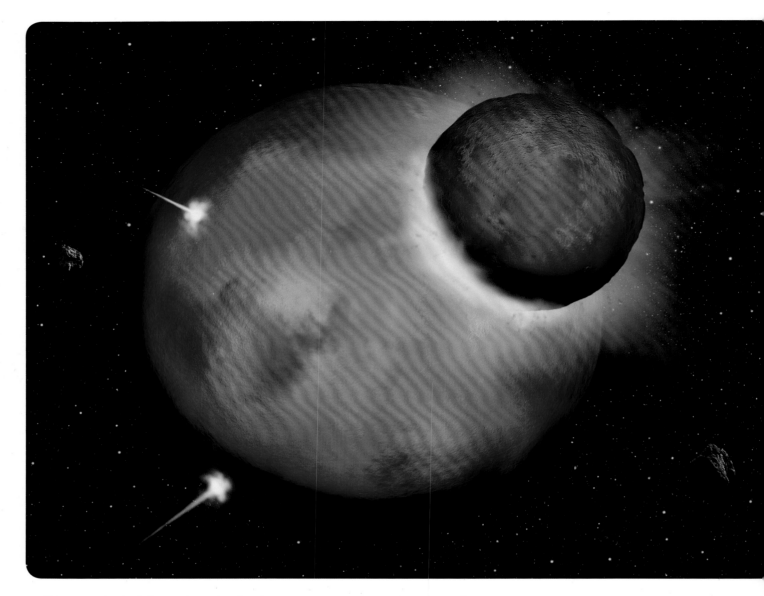

Using computer simulations and samples of lunar rocks, astronomers have figured out that the moon formed out of the material left behind by a collision (just beginning in art above) between Earth and a Mars-size object some 4.5 billion years ago.

Earth formed about 4.6 billion years ago out of a gigantic star explosion that gave birth to the sun and the rest of the solar system. As rocky debris rained down on the planet's young molten surface, an unexpected cosmic collision suddenly changed everything. Around 4.5 billion years ago, an object about the size of Mars slammed

When the object hit the molten Earth (art above), the material that was knocked off first stabilized into a ring of molten rock, then fused back together, and eventually re-formed into the moon we see today. In the early solar system, collisions like this happened all the time.

into Earth, tilting it 23.5 degrees on its axis. This collision also knocked off a big chunk of the planet. The chunk broke into pieces and formed a gigantic ring around Earth. The pieces, still hot and molten, quickly came back together and formed the moon. This may explain why the moon's composition is nearly identical to that of the Earth's crust.

Once formed, the moon helped stabilize the rotation of Earth. That's one of the lucky events that made it possible for life to survive here. If Earth were spinning upright on its axis, the Equator would heat up much more than it does today. We would have no change of seasons, and the weather on our planet would be much more severe.

A WET WORLD

As Earth and the moon began the long process of cooling down, changes took place on the planet. Erupting volcanoes released water vapor that formed into clouds. The clouds quickly returned water to the surface as rain. Comets still raining down on the surface also brought in staggering amounts of water that slowly filled basins. Gradually, Earth's surface was completely covered with one global salty ocean averaging two miles (3.2 km) deep. Biologists believe life first began in these warm, salty oceans.

ABOUT 3.5 BILLION YEARS AGO Earth was covered by one gigantic reddish ocean, whose color came from hydrocarbons. The first life on Earth were simple bacteria that could live without oxygen. These bacteria released large amounts of methane gas into an atmosphere that would have been poisonous to us.

ABOUT THREE BILLION YEARS AGO something new appeared in the global ocean. Erupting volcanoes linked together to form larger land-masses. A new form of life also appeared—blue-green algae, the first living thing that used energy from the sun.

TWO BILLION YEARS AGO these algae filled the air with oxygen, killing off the methane-producing bacteria. Colored pools of greenish-brown plant life floated on the ocean waters. The oxygen revolution that would someday make human life possible was now underway.

ABOUT 530 MILLION YEARS AGO, the Cambrian explosion occurred. It's called an explosion because it's the time when most major animal groups first appeared in our fossil records. Back then, Earth was a place of swamps, seas, a few active volcanoes, and oceans teeming with strange life.

MORE THAN 450 MILLION YEARS AGO, life began moving from the oceans onto dry land. About 200 million years later, along came the dinosaurs. For more than 150 million years, they would dominate life on Earth.

Over time, landmasses thrust up by volcanic activity began to rise out of Earth's oceans. These landmasses began to drift and collide, growing larger and larger until they formed a giant supercontinent called Rodinia about 425 million years ago. Rodinia eventually broke apart into smaller continents. About 225 million years ago the smaller continents pushed together again to form Pangaea. Slowly, after another 94 million years, that supercontinent separated into the continents we see today.

Even today, the continents are drifting. Scientists predict that 250 million years from now North America will collide with Africa, and South America will wrap around the southern tip of Africa. By then, the Pacific Ocean will cover half of Earth.

The idea that the solid ground we are standing on may be slowly moving is difficult to believe. Even more amazing is that the interior structure of Earth is still pretty much a big mystery to us. Scientists believe the structure of Earth consists of four separate layers. Covering the outer surface, the part where we build houses and plant trees, is the rocky crust. It averages five miles (8 km) thick under the oceans and up to 45 miles (72 km) thick under the continents. If Earth were the size of an apple, the crust would be about the thickness of the apple peel.

Rodinia
425 million years ago

Pangaea
225 million years ago

94 million years ago

Today

The surface of Earth is always changing. The crust is made up of plates that move slowly, carrying the oceans and continents with them.

Exosphere

Thermosphere

Ionosphere

Mesosphere

Stratosphere

Troposphere

Our layered atmosphere (art above) is composed mostly of nitrogen and oxygen, with small amounts of carbon dioxide and other gases mixed with water vapor. All weather occurs in the lowest level, the troposphere.

In 1970, Soviet scientists began trying to drill through the crust. They only succeeded in digging a hole about a third of the way through it before they gave up. It took them two decades to drill down 7.6 miles (12 km). Even though they did not make it beyond the crust, what they found surprised them. First, the temperatures down there were hot enough to cook a turkey or bake a pie! And, the rock at that depth was saturated with water — something nobody believed was possible.

Below the crust is the mantle, a layer of dense, semisolid rock. It flows out through cracks onto the surface as lava when volcanoes erupt. Beneath the mantle is a liquid outer core that spins like a motor, generating a magnetic field around Earth that repels damaging solar radiation. At the center of our planet is a solid core, where the temperatures may reach 9000°F (5000°C)—about as hot as the surface of the sun.

EARTH'S ATMOSPHERE

Today, Earth's atmosphere is nearly 80 percent nitrogen and 21 percent oxygen, with traces of carbon dioxide, water, and argon. The small amount of carbon dioxide in the atmosphere helps moderate the temperatures of our planet. If there were too little carbon dioxide, Earth would become too cold, too much and it would grow unbearably hot.

Unlike any other place that we know of in our solar system, the oxygen in our atmosphere is provided and replenished by living organisms. Plant life on Earth "exhales" oxygen that

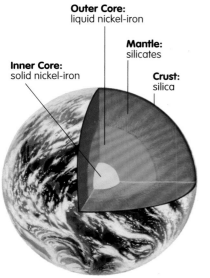

Outer Core: liquid nickel-iron

Mantle: silicates

Inner Core: solid nickel-iron

Crust: silica

A thin layer of cooled rock, Earth's crust supports the oceans and the continental plates. Just beneath the crust lies the molten rock of the mantle, the origin of lava, and beneath that two layers of core.

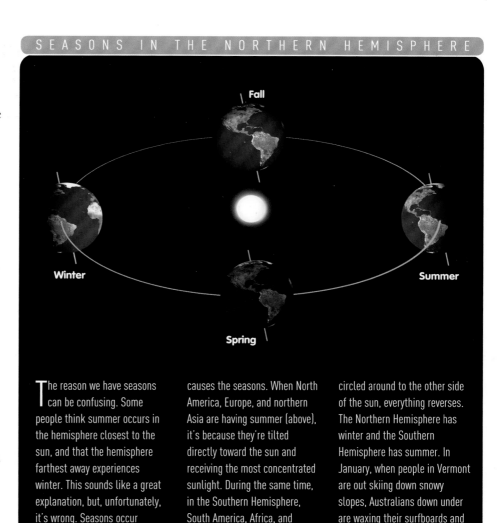

Fall

Winter

Summer

Spring

The reason we have seasons can be confusing. Some people think summer occurs in the hemisphere closest to the sun, and that the hemisphere farthest away experiences winter. This sounds like a great explanation, but, unfortunately, it's wrong. Seasons occur because Earth tilts 23.5 degrees on its axis. That tilt affects the intensity of the sunlight hitting the surface, and that in turn causes the seasons. When North America, Europe, and northern Asia are having summer (above), it's because they're tilted directly toward the sun and receiving the most concentrated sunlight. During the same time, in the Southern Hemisphere, South America, Africa, and Australia are tilted away from the sun, so sunlight is less concentrated and there's less heat. Six months later, when Earth has circled around to the other side of the sun, everything reverses. The Northern Hemisphere has winter and the Southern Hemisphere has summer. In January, when people in Vermont are out skiing down snowy slopes, Australians down under are waxing their surfboards and sunbathing on the beach.

animals need. Without plants, there would be no animal life. In turn, animals exhale carbon dioxide that plants use in photosynthesis.

Earth's atmosphere has no definite boundary. It just becomes thinner as it fades into outer space. The atmosphere is divided into layers. The layer closest to the ground is called the troposphere. It extends about eight miles (13 km) into the sky.

This is the layer where all weather occurs and where most planes fly. Above the troposphere is the stratosphere, which continues out to about 30 miles (50 km) above the surface. In the lower stratosphere is the very important ozone layer. A special form of oxygen, ozone blocks deadly ultraviolet radiation from the sun. Without it, plants and animals wouldn't survive.

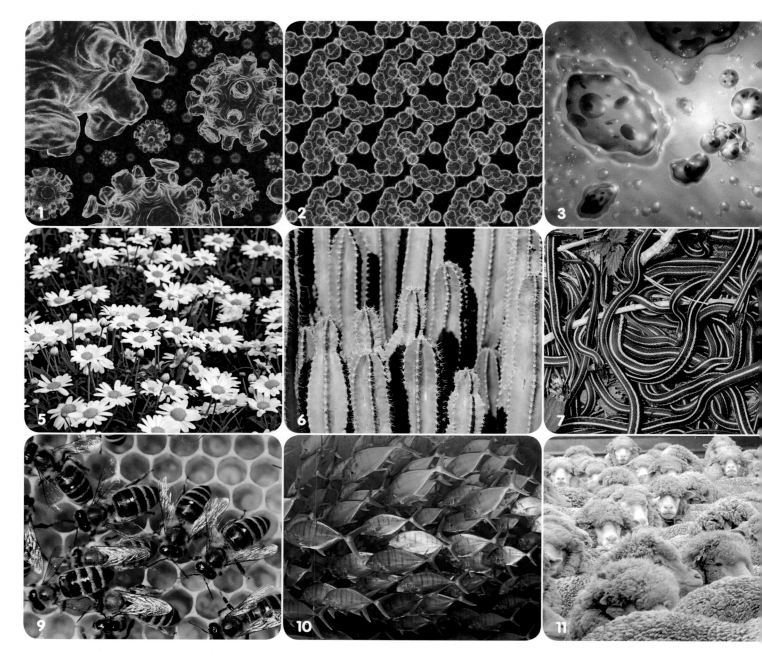

Living things are found everywhere on Earth, from the tropical Equator to the frozen Poles, from the bottom of the oceans to the tops of mountains, inside other organisms (including us) and inside scalding volcanic sulfur pools. The diversity and distribution of life on Earth are staggering. From amoebas to elephants, electric eels to butterflies, scientists have yet to catalogue all of the species of life existing here on our planet. Taxonomists, the scientists who try to group life forms into similar categories, have identified about 1.2 million distinct animal and plant species, mostly mammals and birds. But it's estimated that the number of undiscovered species—mostly fish, fungi, insects, and land animals—is about eight million. (This total does not include simple organisms such as bacteria.) Scientists say that if you want to discover a new animal, all you have to do is spend a day in a tropical rain forest in South America, looking under a log or a rock.

Scientists are not quite sure how life began on Earth, but they're fairly certain where it

began—in the sea. Most living creatures, including human beings, carry the fossil record of this past inside them. Since 71 percent of Earth is covered by water, and our bodies are about 60 percent water, in a way we are walking containers of ocean.

The earliest life on Earth probably looked like the bacteria we find everywhere on the planet today. Over the past 3.7 billion years, organisms on Earth have diversified and adapted to almost every environment imaginable. How they did this is still unknown. Has this same process occurred elsewhere in our solar system or on other planets circling distant stars?

Within the next 25 years, we may well have an answer to this question.

Life on Earth is as beautiful as it is diverse. The photographs above are just a sampling. (The first four are tiny organisms seen under a microscope.)

1 an influenza virus
2 bacteria cells
3 amoeba
4 phytoplankton
5 a field of daisies
6 desert cacti
7 garter snakes
8 a flock of geese
9 honeybees inside their hive
10 a school of pilot fish
11 a herd of sheep
12 different kinds of coral
13 people gathered for a football game

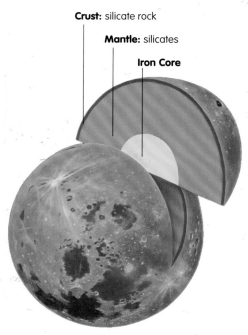

Crust: silicate rock

Mantle: silicates

Iron Core

The moon has far less iron than Earth, which helps explain why its density is only one-sixth that of Earth's.

The moon is our closest companion in space. Only three days away by spacecraft, it's a dramatic reminder of how violent and chaotic the early solar system was. With just a pair of binoculars, we can see how the moon's terrain was smoothed by the lava flows of ancient volcanoes or scarred with impact craters a hundred miles (160 km) in diameter.

Earth's atmosphere causes most space objects to burn up before impact, but the moon has no atmosphere. Everything heading for it hits its surface. None of these impact scars is erased over time by the actions of weather. The footprints left by the Apollo astronauts in 1969 will remain on the moon's surface for at least another ten million years.

There are two types of terrain on the moon: the deeply cratered highlands and the relatively smooth lowlands called "maria," from *mare,* the Latin word for "sea." Maria are found mostly on the near side that faces Earth. They formed four billion years ago, when asteroids smashed into the moon, causing lava to flow out and resurface vast areas. The far side of the moon either missed being hit or the crust there is thicker and kept lava from reaching the surface.

SOLAR AND LUNAR ECLIPSES

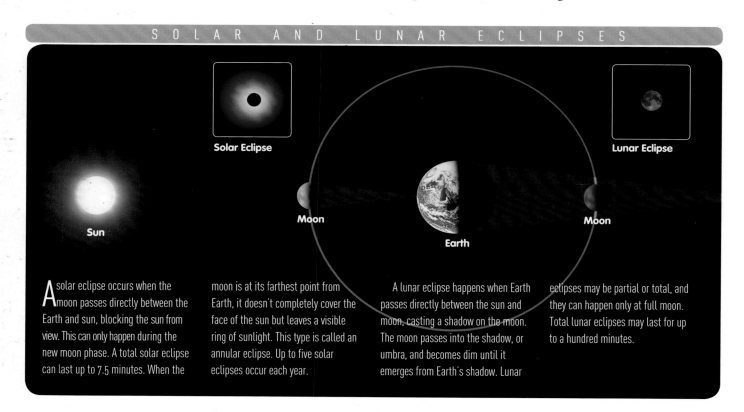

Solar Eclipse

Lunar Eclipse

Sun

Moon

Earth

Moon

A solar eclipse occurs when the moon passes directly between the Earth and sun, blocking the sun from view. This can only happen during the new moon phase. A total solar eclipse can last up to 7.5 minutes. When the moon is at its farthest point from Earth, it doesn't completely cover the face of the sun but leaves a visible ring of sunlight. This type is called an annular eclipse. Up to five solar eclipses occur each year.

A lunar eclipse happens when Earth passes directly between the sun and moon, casting a shadow on the moon. The moon passes into the shadow, or umbra, and becomes dim until it emerges from Earth's shadow. Lunar eclipses may be partial or total, and they can happen only at full moon. Total lunar eclipses may last for up to a hundred minutes.

If you were standing on the moon like these astronauts (art right), and the Earth moved in front of the sun, you would observe a solar eclipse almost twenty minutes in length. Sunlight, passing through the edge of Earth's atmosphere, would cast an eerie red glow over the lunar landscape.

Like Earth, the moon has mountain ranges. Many are found along the edges of large craters, where the impacts of asteroids suddenly thrust them up. One of the biggest surprises for the Apollo astronauts was that the mountains of the moon are not sharp and jagged but soft and rounded. Since the moon doesn't have an atmosphere, there are only dark black shadows on its surface, not the soft gray ones we have on Earth. Because of this, and because there are no familiar objects like telephone poles, it is impossible for astronauts standing on the moon to tell whether a mountain is large and distant or small and close by.

The gravitational forces of Earth and the moon pull on each other. This causes some interesting results, including the tides along our shorelines. When the moon formed more than four billion years ago, it was six times closer to us than it is today. Over time, it has edged away in its orbit. Now it takes the same amount of time—28 days—for the moon to rotate once on its axis and to revolve around Earth. This is called tidal lock, and it's the reason we only see one side of the moon. Most of the larger moons in the solar system are in tidal lock with their planets, too.

About five billion years from now, Earth will gain a ring system as the moon breaks apart. Earth and its moon will be reunited when lunar debris rains down from the burning heavens (art left).

The moon is still moving away from the Earth, adding 1.5 inches (3.8 cm) a year to its orbit. It won't ever leave the Earth and float away, though— the solar system will end before that could happen.

HUMANS ON THE MOON

NASA plans to return to the moon within the next 20 years. Since its gravitational force is only a sixth of the Earth's, visiting astronauts weigh less there. A 100-pound (45-kg) person would weigh only 16.6 pounds (7.5 kg), and a solidly hit baseball could speed along at 10 miles (16 km) per hour.

Astronaut Buzz Aldrin described the moon as a world of "magnificent desolation." It offers no oxygen to breathe and no global magnetic field to protect it from deadly solar radiation.

THE MOON'S FUTURE

The moon was created out of an ancient collision, and scientists believe it is headed for further catastrophe. In about five billion years, the sun will enter its red giant phase and begin to expand in diameter. As it reaches the orbit of the moon, it will push the moon's orbital path back in toward Earth. Eventually, this will tear the moon apart. At first, the lunar pieces will create a rather lumpy ring system around our planet, then they will crash onto Earth's surface.

The first stars are just beginning to glow in the young universe.

TO THE STARS AND BEYOND

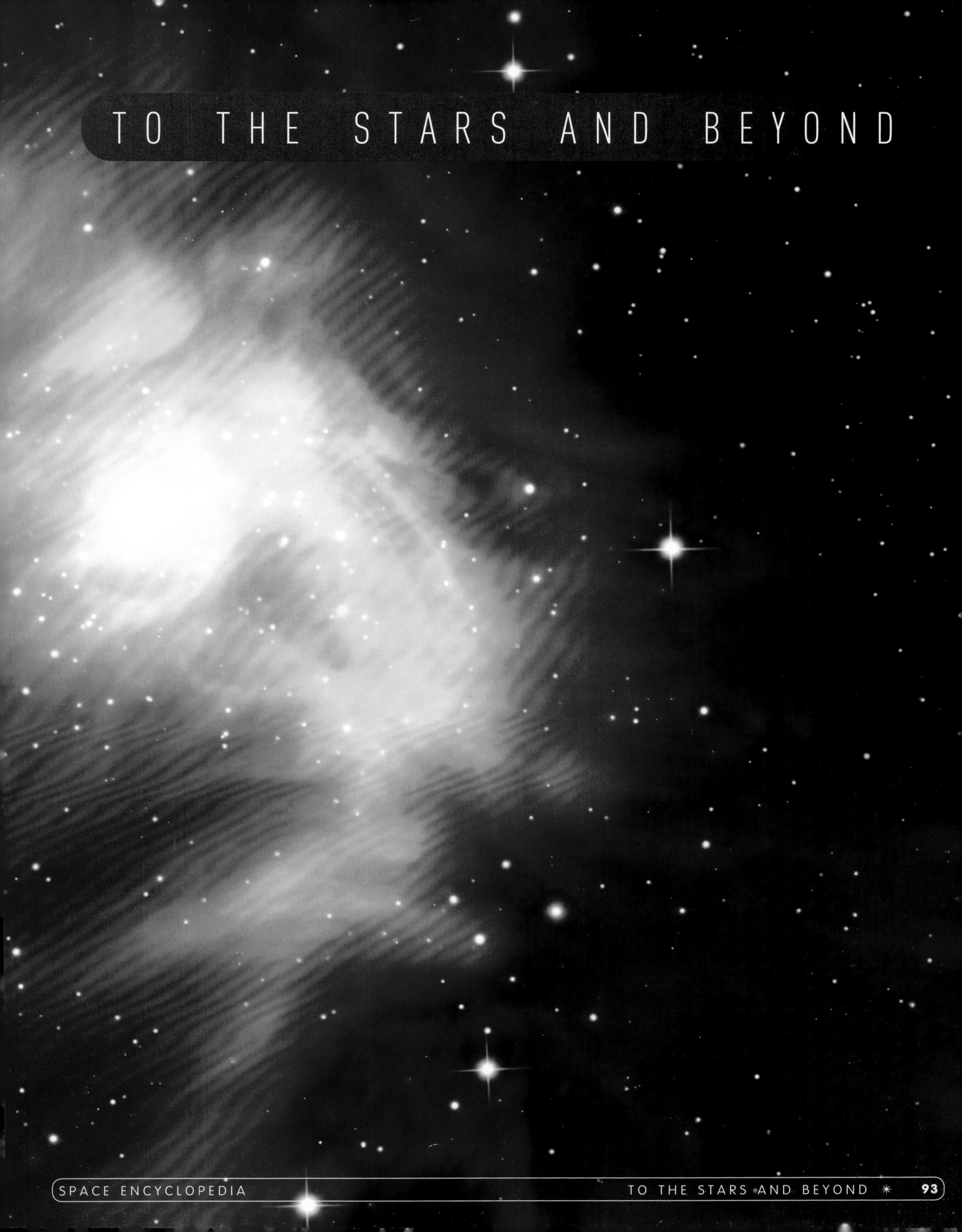

If you're on a dark countryside hill some night, look up at the heavens. Arcing overhead, you may see a faint band of light that looks like milk spilled across the sky. The ancient Romans called that band the *via lactea,* which means the "milky road" or "milky way." The name has stuck for 2,000 years.

A lot of people around the world use the term Milky Way, but some cultures have different names for the band of light. In China, it's called the silver river, and people of the Kalahari Desert in southern Africa call it the backbone of the night.

In 1610, Galileo and his telescope finally revealed that this band was actually made up of stars. We now know that there are hundreds of billions of them in our galaxy. Even on a clear night, though, the average person can see only about 2,000 with the naked eye. The Milky Way also has dark patches sprinkled through it. Those patches aren't areas without stars. They're clouds of interstellar dust that block the light from the stars behind them.

Meteors slash across the pristine night sky on Easter Island in the southern Pacific Ocean, far from distracting city lights. Here, our Milky Way galaxy shines brightly overhead with visible dark dust clouds obscuring parts of the galactic center, while other areas glow by reflected starlight radiating from billions of distant suns.

Long ago, people looking at the sky noticed that some stars made shapes and patterns. By playing connect-the-dots, they imagined people and animals in the sky. Their legendary heroes and monsters were pictured in the stars.

Today, we call these star patterns constellations. There are 88 constellations in all. Some are only visible when you're north of the Equator, and others only south of it.

The ones visible in the Southern Hemisphere, such as the Southern Cross, have names given them by European ocean voyagers. In the 16th-century Age of Exploration, their ships began visiting southern lands. Astronomers used the star observations of these navigators to fill in the blank spots on their celestial maps.

Constellations aren't fixed in the sky. The star arrangement that makes up each one would look different from another location in the universe. Constellations also change over time, because every star we see is moving through space. Over thousands of years, the stars in the Big Dipper, which is part of the larger constellation Ursa Major (the Great Bear), will move so far apart that the dipper pattern will disappear.

Centered on Polaris, the North Star, the time-lapse photograph at the top shows how stars seem to spin around the sky as the Earth spins on its axis. Our ancestors imagined people and animals in star patterns, as in the constellation wheel to the left.

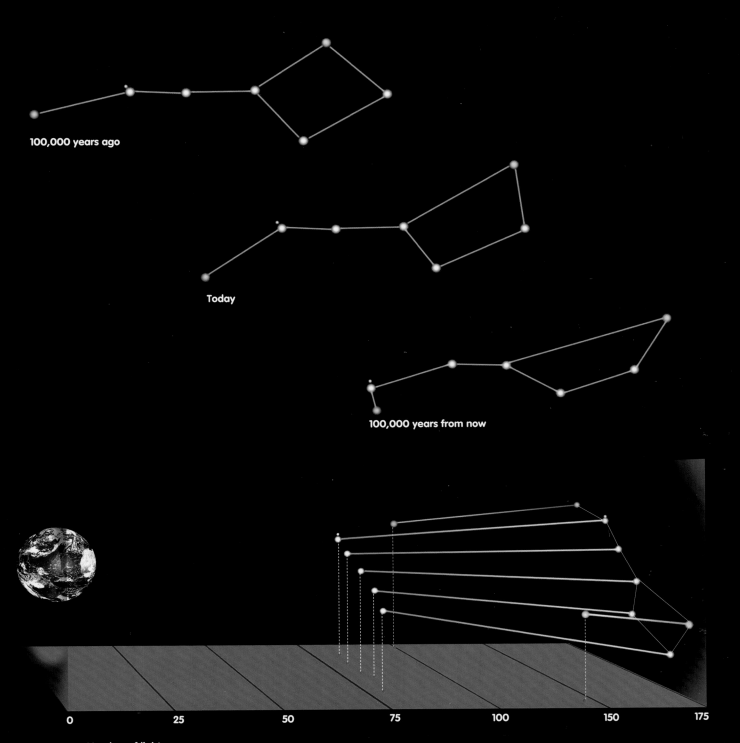

100,000 years ago

Today

100,000 years from now

Number of light-years away

| 0 | 25 | 50 | 75 | 100 | 150 | 175 |

Constellations are always changing because stars move through space. The Big Dipper looked more like a square in the past. In the future it will flatten (art top).

When we look up at the sky, the stars that seem to form patterns along a flat plane and to be close together may actually be in very different locations in space. Some stars in the Big Dipper are twice as far away from us as others (art bottom).

A telescope is a time machine, but a time machine that only takes you into the past. That's because a telescope shows things in the sky not as they are now but as they were.

To understand this, remember that a telescope collects light from the heavens. It takes time for that light to reach us, even moving at 186,000 miles (300,000 km) per second—the speed of light. Light from the sun reaches Earth in eight minutes, so we see the sun as it looked eight minutes ago. Light from Pluto takes about four hours to reach us because it has to cross three billion miles (five billion km) of space.

BIG DISTANCES

Once you move beyond the solar system, the distances get unbelievably big. In one Earth year, light travels six trillion miles. The closest star to the sun, Alpha Centauri, is 24 trillion miles (41 trillion km) away. The center of the Milky Way is 125 thousand trillion miles away.

The numbers get so big that astronomers have created a word to describe cosmic distances: the light-year. One light-year is the distance light travels in an Earth year, so a light-year equals six trillion miles (10 trillion km). Since light from Alpha Centauri takes four years to reach us, we say that Alpha Centauri lies four light-years away.

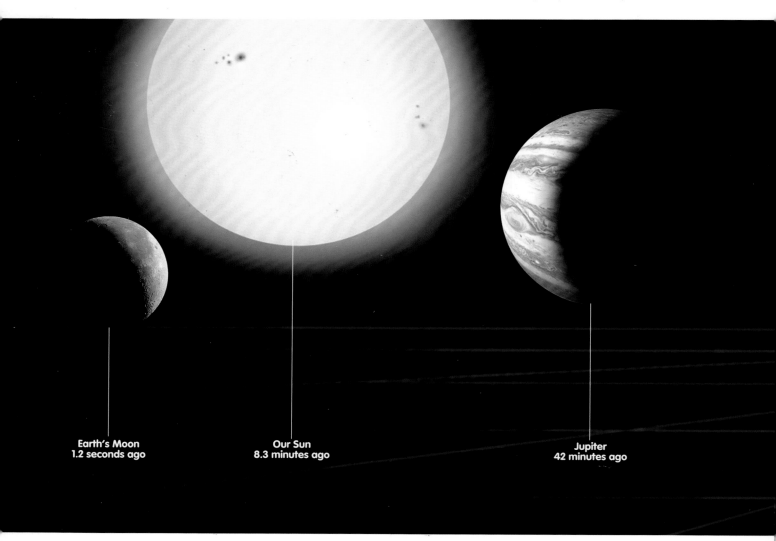

Earth's Moon
1.2 seconds ago

Our Sun
8.3 minutes ago

Jupiter
42 minutes ago

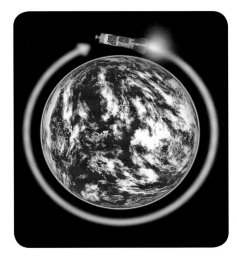

If you could shine a flashlight around Earth, its light beam would circle the planet more than seven times in one second because that is the speed that light travels. The much slower space shuttle circled Earth once every hour and a half.

LOOK-BACK TIME

Look-back time is how far back in time we are seeing something in the sky. The look-back time for Alpha Centauri is four years. The red star Aldebaran in the constellation Taurus is about 65 light-years away, so it has a look-back time of 65 years. Looking at Aldebaran, we see that star as it was 65 years ago. It's like looking at pictures of your grandparents when they were just children.

The travel time of light gets even longer when you look outside the Milky Way galaxy.

For example, the closest large galaxy to us is the Andromeda spiral galaxy, 2.5 million light-years away. The light we see from Andromeda left there when the earliest ancestors of humans first appeared on Earth more than three million years ago.

A telescope is like a time machine because it allows us to see things as they were in the past. Light from the sun takes about 8 minutes 20 seconds to arrive at Earth, so we see the sun as it was 8.3 minutes ago.

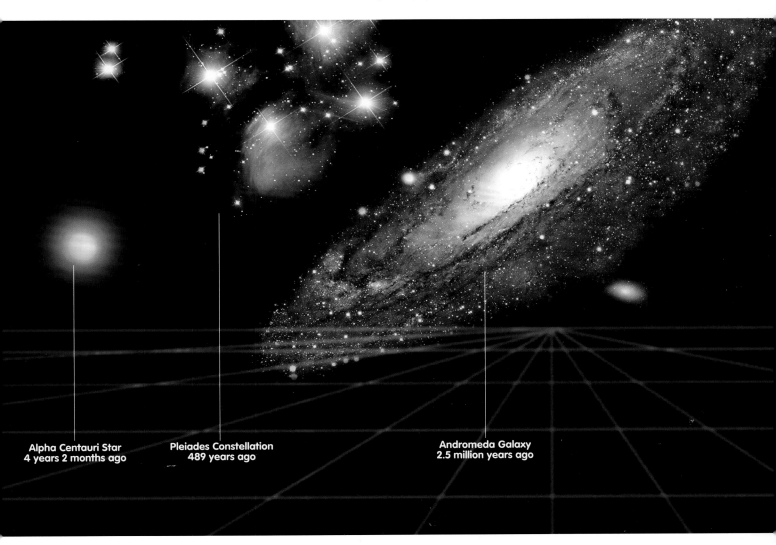

Alpha Centauri Star
4 years 2 months ago

Pleiades Constellation
489 years ago

Andromeda Galaxy
2.5 million years ago

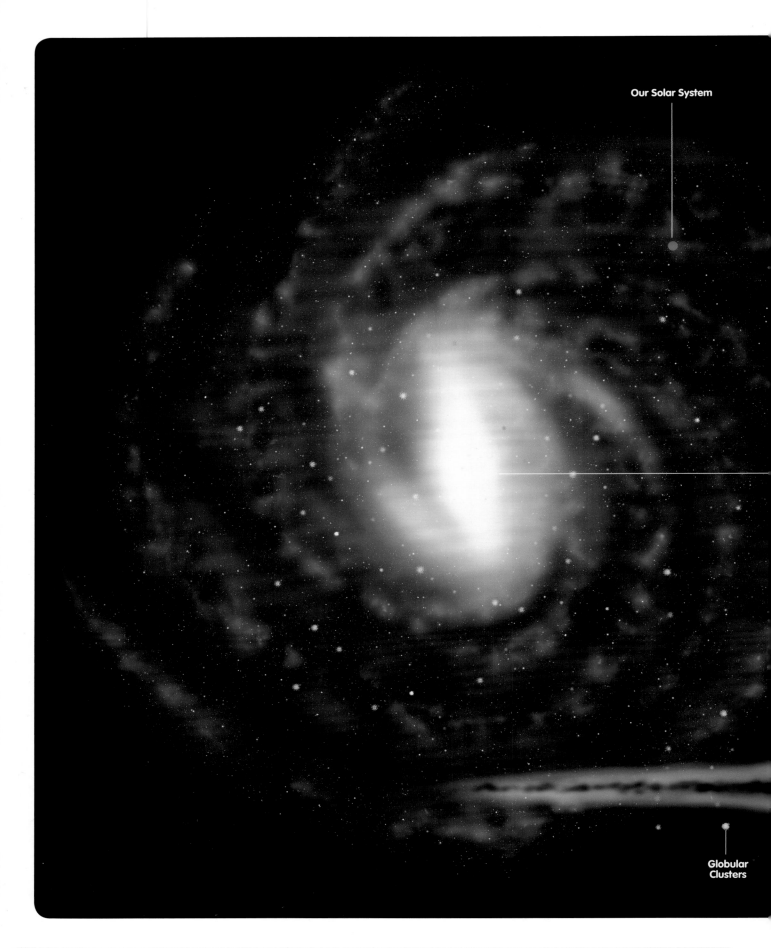

Our Solar System

Globular
Clusters

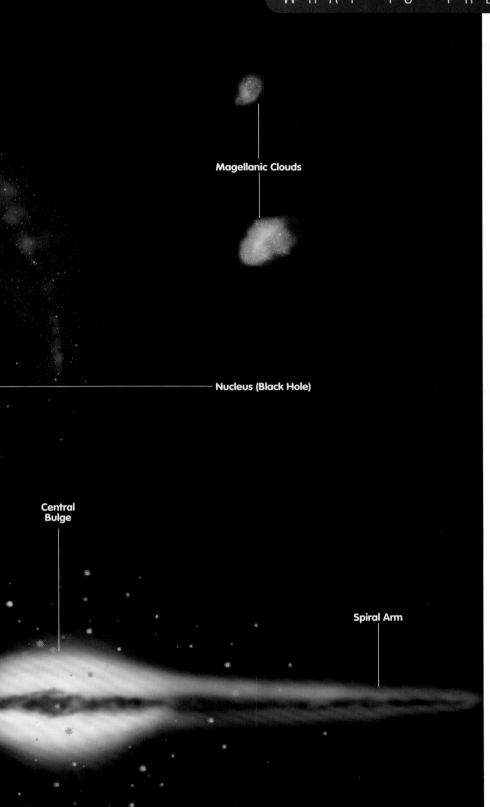

Magellanic Clouds

Nucleus (Black Hole)

Central
Bulge

Spiral Arm

Our galaxy, the Milky Way, appears to be a band of stars in the sky, but it's actually a disk. Hundreds of billions of stars are clumped into lines called spiral arms because they spiral outward. When we look up at the night sky, we're seeing the edge of the disk, like the side of a Frisbee.

Earth is located about halfway between the center of the Milky Way and its outer edge, in one of the spiral arms. Light from the galaxy's center takes 25,000 light-years to reach us.

Our solar system orbits the galactic center about once every 230 million years. The last time we were on this side of the Milky Way, the earliest dinosaurs were just starting to emerge.

At the galaxy's center, frequent star explosions fry huge sections of space. Those explosions would wipe out any life on nearby planets. We're lucky that Earth is located where it is, far away from the center.

Our Milky Way galaxy (art left) has a bulge in its middle that surrounds the galactic center, or nucleus. In the nucleus is a giant black hole. The central bulge is surrounded by a flat disk. Within the disk, spiral arms of stars and gas wrap around the center. Outside the disk, globular star clusters orbit like swarms of bees. Companion galaxies called the Magellanic Clouds also pass by the Milky Way.

The Milky Way may look like a peaceful, static arrangement of sparkling lights in our night sky, but it's really like a bustling restaurant kitchen, always cooking up something new. And stars are its main dish.

New stars form continually. In our galaxy, most of the action takes place in the spiral arms, which contain plenty of hydrogen gas to make stars. On average only a few stars are born every year in the Milky Way. Our galaxy is getting older, though, and the rate of star birth is slowing down.

The births and deaths of stars are linked. When stars die, their remains mix with the remains of other stars over time to create new stars—or new solar systems.

Stars aren't the only things that are changing. Galaxies are moving through space, sometimes bumping into each other and re-forming. Scientists even think new universes might be forming and re-forming.

The birth and death of stars are amazing sights to see. This bright background image is a young star field in the constellation Monoceros. The bright blue-white stars in the picture are babies—just starting to shine. The inset shows a dying star that is expanding into a huge shell of gas as it strews its stardust back into space. The Hubble telescope captured both of these images.

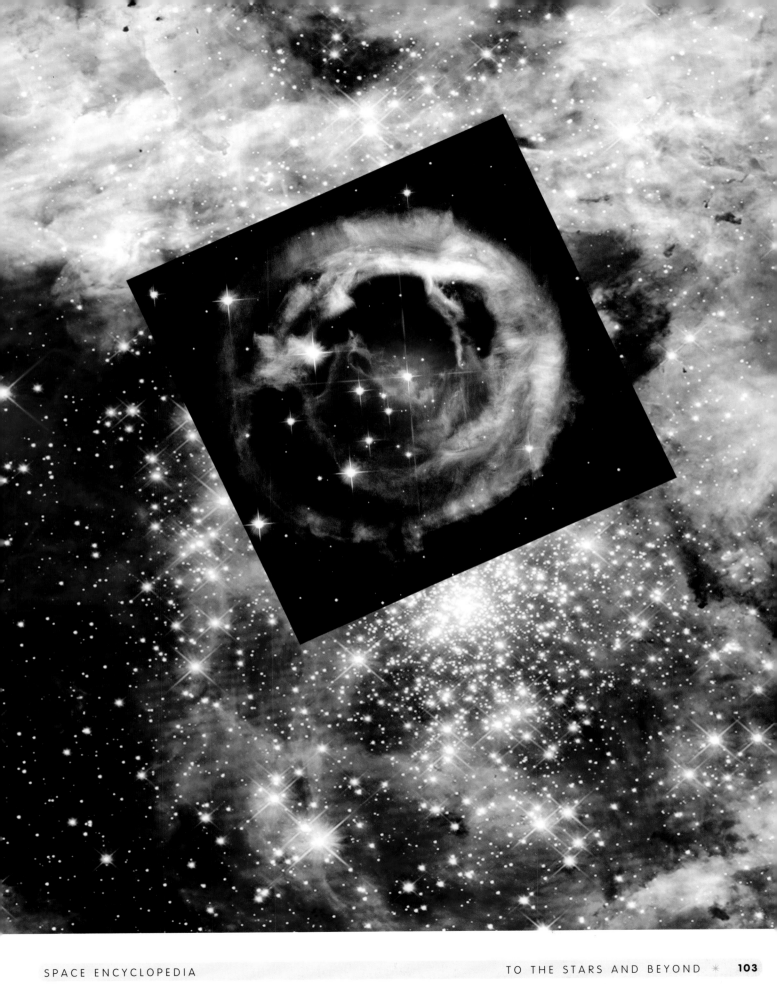

Poets might say that the stars are forever, but scientists know that's not true. All stars eventually die when they run out of fuel.

You might think a more massive star would live longer because it has more fuel to burn. But the heavier a star is, the faster it burns through its fuel, and the shorter its lifetime is. The most massive stars will live for only a few million years, whereas the least massive stars can live for trillions of years.

All stars spend most of their lives fusing hydrogen and turning it into helium in their cores. This nuclear fusion creates the energy we see as starlight. Eventually, the star's core runs out of hydrogen. This is the end for low-mass stars like our sun.

When higher-mass stars run out of hydrogen, they can start fusing the helium in their cores, creating carbon and oxygen. The most massive stars can keep fusing heavier and heavier elements until their core is full of hot, dense iron. That's the end of the road, because no energy comes from fusing iron.

All stars come from nebulas (top left in art right), but then their lives take different courses to their final end. Smaller stars (top row) end as tiny, dead white dwarfs. But the more massive stars (bottom row) explode as supernovas and leave behind crushing black holes or neutron stars.

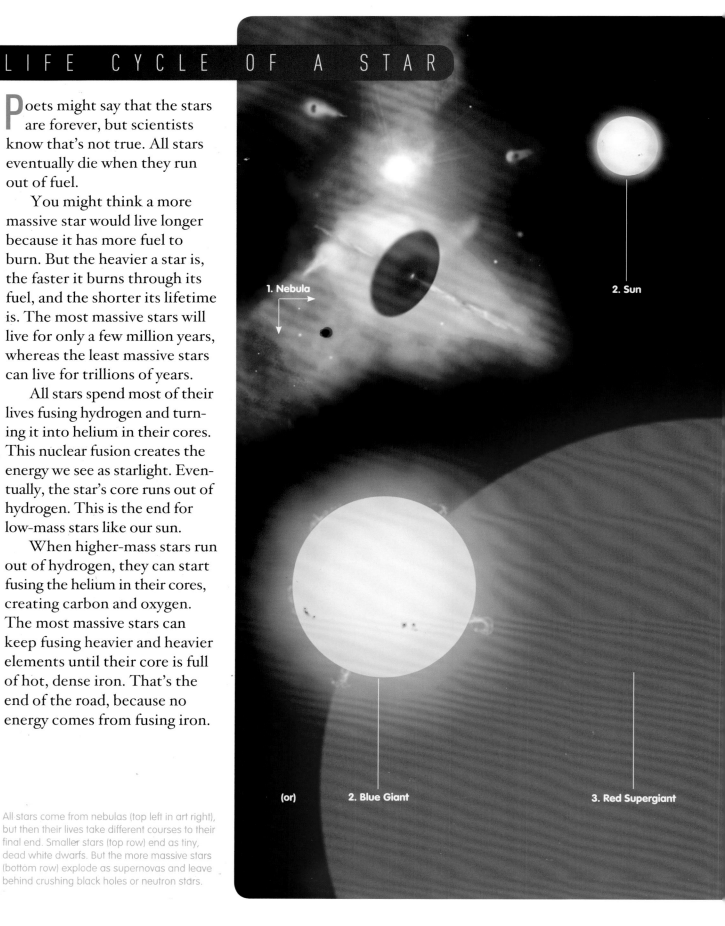

1. Nebula

2. Sun

(or)   2. Blue Giant   3. Red Supergiant

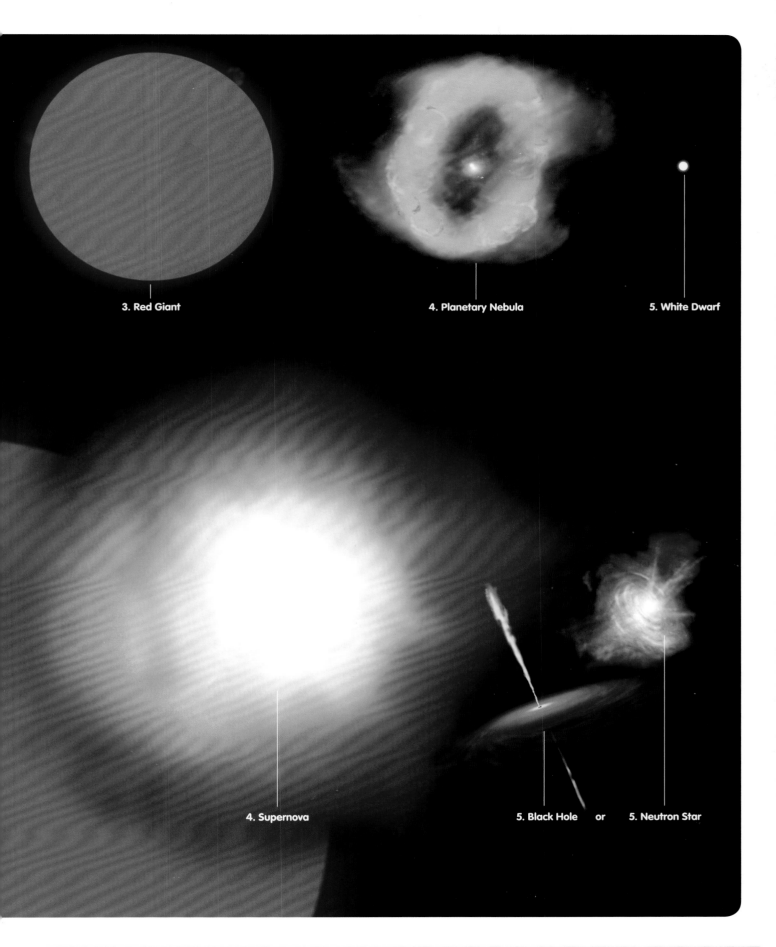

3. Red Giant

4. Planetary Nebula

5. White Dwarf

4. Supernova

5. Black Hole   or   5. Neutron Star

A star is born inside an enormous cloud of gases, of which hydrogen is the main one. This gas cloud is called a nebula. As clumps in a nebula attract more gas, they grow larger and hotter until they ignite and become stars.

Newborn stars light up the surrounding nebula the way car headlights light up the fog. A long-exposure photograph reveals a nebula's true colors, but in a telescope, it glows an eerie grayish green. Many backyard astronomers look for nebulas, using a list compiled by French astronomer Charles Messier.

These photographs show three nebulas in the Messier catalogue. In each photo, the nebula is the glowing reddish formation near the center.

M42 (photo right, top) the Orion Nebula is the most well-known and easy-to-find nebula on Messier's list. It's visible to the unaided eye as the middle point of light in the sword of the constellation Orion, hanging below his belt, where the red X is in the circled diagram. The Orion Nebula contains hundreds of young stars, including a famous grouping of four bright stars called the Trapezium.

M17 (photo right, bottom) The Swan, or Omega Nebula, is located 5,000 light-years from Earth in the constellation Sagittarius. The nebula contains enough hydrogen to make hundreds of stars like our sun.

Many nebulas that are easy to find with telescopes have several names. For example, the Orion Nebula is also called Messier 42, abbreviated M42. The Orion Nebula was the 42nd object on a list compiled by legendary astronomer Charles Messier.

Born in 1730, Charles Messier (top left) was a comet hunter in France. At the age of 14, the teenager became hooked on astronomy when an amazing, six-tailed comet appeared in the sky. When he was in his early 20s, he got his first job as an astronomer.

The only telescopes available to Messier were fairly small, and lots of different objects looked similar in them. It was easy to confuse a comet with a nebula or a galaxy. They all looked like faint fuzz balls in the telescope eyepiece.

To help clear up the confusion, Messier began keeping track of objects that looked like comets but didn't move across the sky the way comets do. He worked from his observatory in Paris (bottom left) and published his first catalogue of 45 objects in 1771. Messier continued to add to the list throughout his lifetime. Eventually, his catalogue grew to 110 objects.

Messier also tracked 20 comets. Although 7 of them were first spotted by others, 13 were seen by Messier before anyone else, and he still gets the credit for them.

Since Messier used telescopes similar to those available to anyone today, backyard astronomers often look for the so-called Messier objects. Some of these enthusiasts even challenge themselves to a "Messier marathon" and try to observe all 110 objects in a single night.

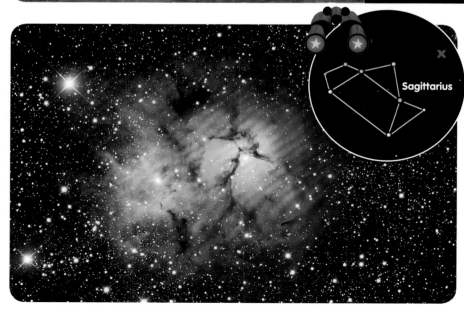

M20 (photo left) The Trifid Nebula gets its name from its three-part appearance. Filaments of dark dust seem to divide it into sections. The red color comes from hot hydrogen gas heated by young stars, while the blue is the usual color of massive young stars.

Astronomers classify stars based on their size, temperature, color, and luminosity. When astronomers talk about the size of a star, they usually

Stars come in a variety of sizes and masses. When they're on the main sequence, they range from hefty, hot O stars to lightweight, cool M stars (art below). As smaller stars like our sun age, they swell in physical size to become red giants, then fade away into dying embers called white dwarfs.

mean the star's mass, or how much "stuff" it contains. This classification system is for young and middle-age stars. The rule changes when stars get old.

A STAR'S PRIME OF LIFE

Scientists say that when a star is in the prime of its life, it is on the "main sequence." That means it's producing energy by converting hydrogen to helium (sidebar below right).

The mass of a star determines everything else about it: how hot it is, what color it is, and how long it will live. Massive stars are hot and blue; small stars are cool and red.

To identify main sequence stars more easily, astronomers assign letters to the different star types. For historical reasons, some of the letters are

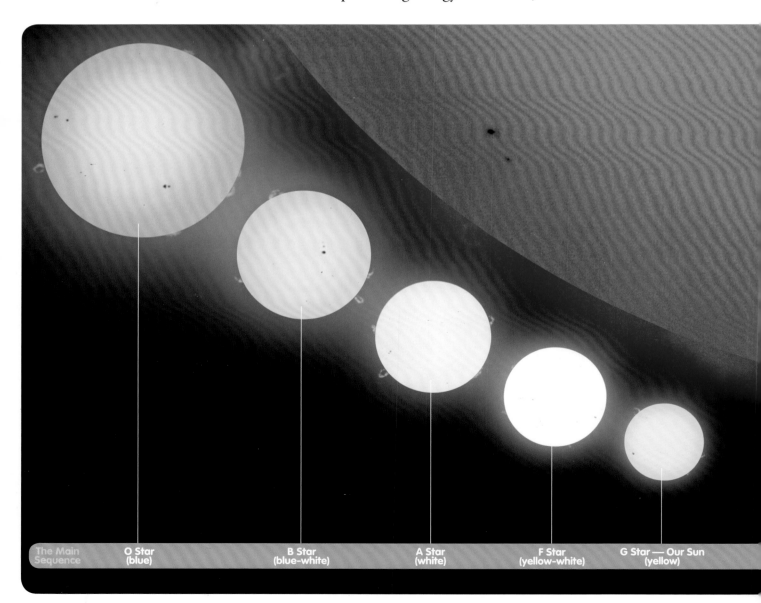

The Main Sequence

O Star (blue)

B Star (blue-white)

A Star (white)

F Star (yellow-white)

G Star — Our Sun (yellow)

skipped, so the labels are not in alphabetical order. Instead, they are O, B, A, F, G, K, and M. The hottest stars are type O, while the coolest are type M.

The smallest stars are about one-tenth the mass of the sun. They're cool, dim, and red. They can live for trillions of years, burning slowly and steadily. The largest stars are about a hundred times the mass of the sun or more. They're hot, bright, and blue. They live fast and die young, burning out in only a few million years.

OLD STARS

A star's size changes as it stops fusing hydrogen and leaves the main sequence. It begins burning hydrogen in a thin shell-like area surrounding its core. Fusion energy from this shell heats the star and makes it swell up, expanding to many times its previous size. Small and medium-size stars, like our sun, expand to be much, much bigger than an O star, but with far less mass. At this stage, they're called red giants. In the end, they fade into white dwarfs.

Large stars become red supergiants. One famous supergiant is the star Betelgeuse in the constellation Orion.

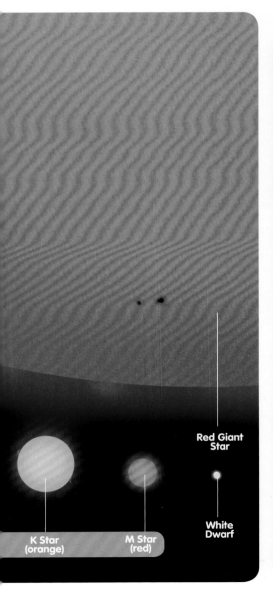

Red Giant Star

White Dwarf

K Star (orange)

M Star (red)

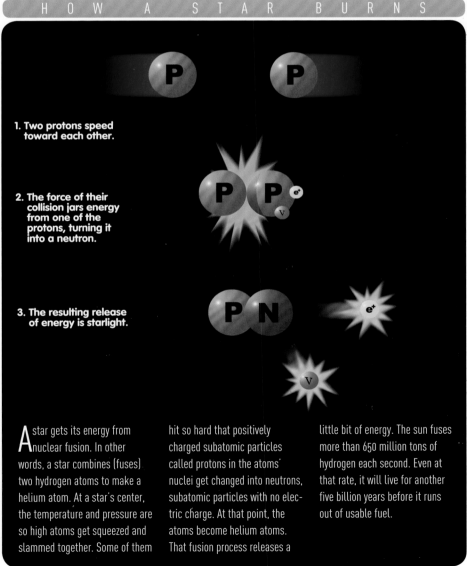

HOW A STAR BURNS

1. Two protons speed toward each other.

2. The force of their collision jars energy from one of the protons, turning it into a neutron.

3. The resulting release of energy is starlight.

A star gets its energy from nuclear fusion. In other words, a star combines (fuses) two hydrogen atoms to make a helium atom. At a star's center, the temperature and pressure are so high atoms get squeezed and slammed together. Some of them hit so hard that positively charged subatomic particles called protons in the atoms' nuclei get changed into neutrons, subatomic particles with no electric charge. At that point, the atoms become helium atoms. That fusion process releases a little bit of energy. The sun fuses more than 650 million tons of hydrogen each second. Even at that rate, it will live for another five billion years before it runs out of usable fuel.

The end of a star like our sun is both beautiful and peaceful. For a short time, it creates a brilliantly glowing, gaseous nebula.

When this kind of star runs out of hydrogen in its core, it begins fusing hydrogen in a shell-like layer that surrounds the core, the way an eggshell surrounds a yolk. Energy from the hydrogen-burning shell heats the star's outer layers, puffing them up. The star becomes a red giant.

These outer layers swell more and more until they blow off completely, leaving behind the star's hot, dead core. That core is called a white dwarf. It lights up the surrounding gas, creating a glowing planetary nebula.

Over the course of about 10,000 years, the gas slowly spreads out until there is not enough left for us to see. The white dwarf gradually cools and fades away as well. All that remains is a cold black dwarf.

Our five-billion-year-old sun (photo below) is a middle-age star. In another five billion years, it will reach its end, puffing off its outer gas layers to form a shining nebula, like those shown at right.

The Dumbbell Nebula, or M27, (photo left) was the first nebula from a dying, sunlike star ever discovered. It's one of the brightest such nebulas in the night sky. The star at the center ejected gas in two cones that we see from the side, giving the nebula its unique shape.

Cygnus

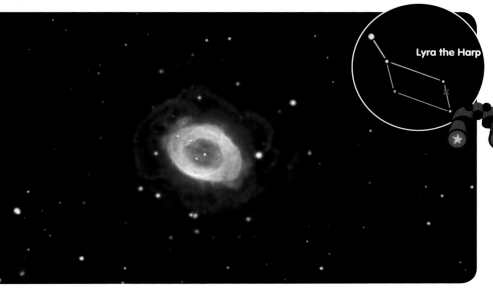

The Ring Nebula, or M57, (photo left) is shaped like the Dumbbell Nebula, with two cones of gas. But from Earth we see the ends of the cones, so the nebula appears ring-shaped. The ring is more than five trillion miles across. It's easy to locate in the constellation of Lyra the Harp.

Lyra the Harp

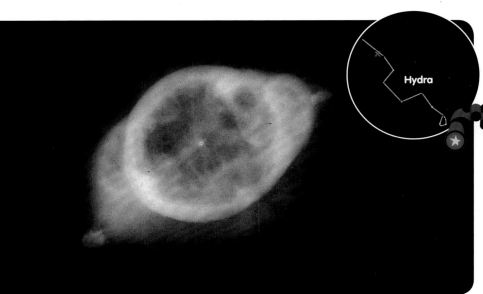

Found in the constellation Hydra, NGC 3242 (photo left) is nicknamed Jupiter's Ghost because it looks similar to that planet in small telescopes. But NGC 3242 is about 1,400 light-years from Earth, much farther away than Jupiter. The NGC in its name stands for New General Catalogue, a list of thousands of objects first published in 1888. The latest version of the NGC was published in 1988 and is now available online for download.

Hydra

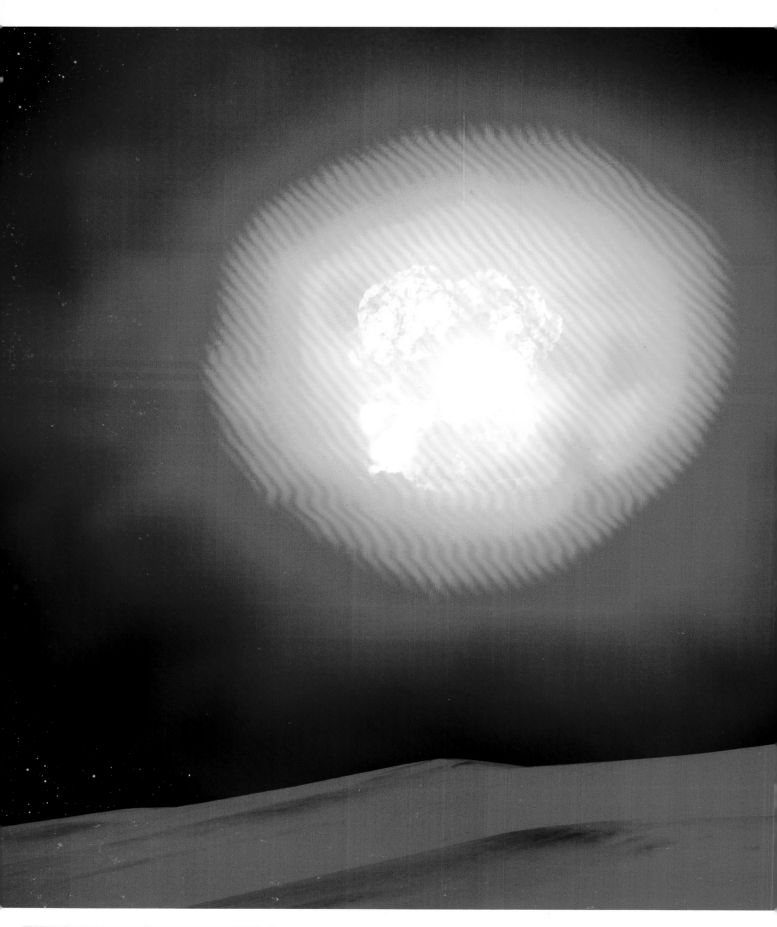

Compared to a medium-size star like our sun, the death of a giant star is dramatic and violent. It actually destroys itself.

Once a massive star runs out of hydrogen in its core, gravity pulls the core inward, making it dense enough and hot enough for its helium to fuse, making carbon and oxygen. That is when the star becomes a red super-giant. Then the carbon and oxygen fuse to make sodium, magnesium, silicon, and heavier elements. The final stage of fusion creates iron.

Fusing iron removes energy rather than releasing it. With no energy source left to push outward against the force of gravity pulling inward, the star's core suddenly collapses. The star's outer layers rush inward, collide, then blast outward again with immense energy. The star explodes into a supernova.

Many of the elements, from helium to iron, that were created in the star's interior are scattered into space, where they can be used by the next generation. The calcium in our bones and the iron in our blood come from ancient supernovas.

In this artwork, a massive star has just exploded as a supernova. The radiation given off from such an explosion would sterilize any planet orbiting the star, leaving behind a dead world.

When a massive star explodes as a supernova, it scatters itself across space. Gas ejected by a supernova rushes out at a speed of millions of miles per hour.

The supernova also creates a shock wave, which slams into surrounding gas ejected by the star before the explosion. That blast wave heats the gas to a temperature of millions of degrees—hot enough to glow. We call that glowing gas cloud a supernova remnant.

A supernova remnant is so hot that it emits high-energy x-ray radiation. Special telescopes are needed to detect and study those x-rays.

A supernova remnant may also emit visible light that we can see with our eyes, or radio waves that can be detected by radio telescopes.

CREATORS AND DESTROYERS

The blast wave of a supernova can rip apart nebulas, but a supernova shock wave can also help new stars form. Interstellar gas compacted by the shock wave may clump together and gather more gas until it ignites as a star.

Taurus

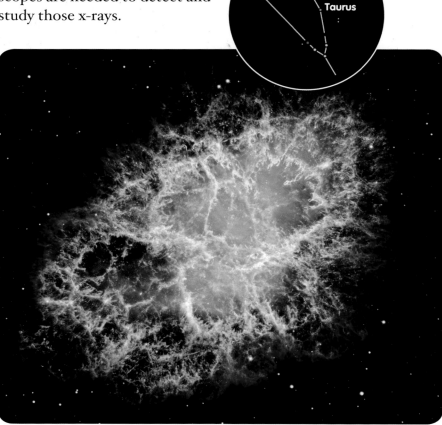

The Crab Nebula, or M1, (photo left) in the constellation Taurus is the only supernova remnant in Messier's catalogue. A star that exploded in the year A.D. 1054 created M1. Sightings of the supernova were recorded in China and possibly in the Americas.

No supernova has been observed in the Milky Way since the invention of the telescope. The next star to go might be Betelgeuse. In the art above, it's shown as a massive red glow consuming the moon (seen faintly toward the top of the art) of a nearby planet (the sphere in the foreground).

Orion

A supernova remnant can become either a black hole (see page 120) or a neutron star.

A neutron star isn't really a star. It's more like a giant atomic nucleus 5–10 miles (8–16 km) across, made entirely of neutrons. Normal atoms are made of three particles—protons, electrons, and neutrons. But the atoms in a supernova core have been squeezed together so tightly that protons and electrons have combined to form neutrons.

Since so much mass is stuffed into such a small sphere, a neutron star is very dense. A sugar cube–size lump would weigh about a billion tons, more than 10,000 aircraft carriers.

PULSARS

Some spinning neutron stars emit beams of radio energy that sweep across space like the beam of a lighthouse or searchlight. If the beam happens to pass over the Earth, we detect a pulsing radio signal every time the beam hits. The neutron stars that create these signals are called pulsars.

As shown in this artwork, the center of the Crab Nebula is a region of powerful energy. Hot gas swirls around a compact pulsar. That pulsar is all that remains of a once-mighty star.

Astronomers didn't always know that pulsars existed. In 1967, astronomer Jocelyn Bell Burnell, then at Cambridge University in England, discovered a strange radio signal coming from outer space that blinked on and off about once every second. She labeled it LGM-1 for "little green men," a joke about possible alien life.

No one really thought that the signal was from aliens, but astronomers weren't sure what was causing it. No steady radio pulses had ever been spotted in the Milky Way before.

Not long after the discovery, a scientist calculated that a spinning neutron star could make radio pulses. The strong magnetic field of a pulsar traps electrons that escaped when the star's core collapsed. Those electrons generate radio waves that are funneled outward by the star's magnetic field into beams of radiation. As the pulsar spins, the beam sweeps across the sky.

Since the discovery of the first pulsar, more than a thousand others have been found. Some spin so fast that they flicker on and off hundreds of times every second.

Astronomers have even found one pulsar that is orbited by three planets. Those planets are cold, barren, and bathed in harsh radiation, so we can be pretty sure no "little green men" live there.

The most powerful super-novas do more than announce the death of a star. They create huge blasts of high-energy radiation called gamma rays. Gamma-ray bursts are the brightest explosions in the universe. They would destroy any life that existed on nearby planets.

A gamma-ray burst has been called the birth cry of a black hole. When a massive star's core collapses, it can form a black hole. If the star was rotating very quickly, a fast-spinning disk of gas will surround the new black hole, and some material from the disk will shoot out in cone-shaped jets. Those jets, coming from deep in the interior of the dying star, will punch through it and rip the rest of the star apart.

A gamma-ray burst (art left) is the most powerful explosion in the universe. The orbiting Fermi Gamma-ray Space Telescope (above) records these cosmic events, which are the result of merging neutron stars and the formation of massive black holes.

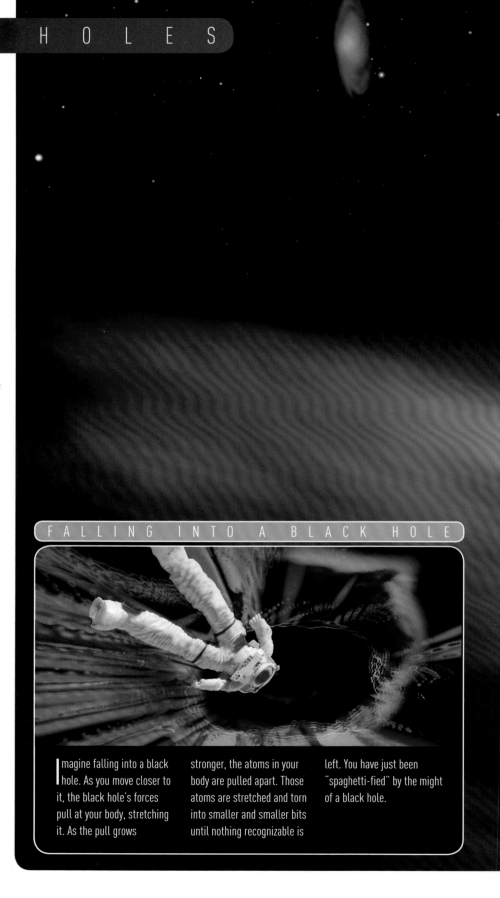

A black hole really seems like a hole in space. Most black holes form when the core of a massive star collapses, crushing itself into oblivion.

A black hole has a stronger gravitational pull than anything else in the universe. It's like a bottomless pit, swallowing whatever gets near enough to it to be pulled in.

Black holes come in different sizes. The smallest has a mass about three times that of the sun. The biggest one scientists have found so far has a mass about 17 billion times the sun's. Really big black holes at the centers of galaxies probably form by swallowing enormous amounts of gas over time.

One of NASA's spacecraft has found thousands of black hole candidates in the Milky Way, but there are probably many more. The nearest one to Earth is about 1,600 light-years away.

The main artwork here shows hydrogen gas from a yellow star (at right in the art) falling into a black hole and forming a disk around it. The two bright white cones are gas that got close to the hole but escaped, thanks to a push from the hole's magnetic field.

FALLING INTO A BLACK HOLE

Imagine falling into a black hole. As you move closer to it, the black hole's forces pull at your body, stretching it. As the pull grows stronger, the atoms in your body are pulled apart. Those atoms are stretched and torn into smaller and smaller bits until nothing recognizable is left. You have just been "spaghetti-fied" by the might of a black hole.

Not every clump in a star-forming nebula will become a star. Sometimes there's not enough gas nearby. Without that fuel, the object never gets dense enough and hot enough to maintain nuclear fusion. Instead, it fizzles.

Our sun contains about a thousand times as much mass as Jupiter. The least massive stars are about 75 times the mass of Jupiter. Anything less massive than that is a failed star.

Astronomers call them brown dwarfs, even though they're not really brown and they're not dwarf stars. They start out at their brightest, then become dimmer and redder than the dimmest star.

BROWN DWARF OR PLANET?

Astronomers are still debating what the difference is between planets and brown dwarfs. Most astronomers think that anything less massive than 13 Jupiters is a planet, whereas anything between 13 and 75 times the mass of Jupiter is a brown dwarf. The lower limit is the mass at which a brown dwarf can briefly fuse a form of hydrogen called deuterium. Planets do not fuse hydrogen at all.

Looking like a glowing red coal, a brown dwarf (art right) is a stellar wannabe without enough mass to sustain nuclear fusion. It is destined to cool off slowly over billions of years, leaving any planets orbiting it in a never-ending deep freeze.

HOW PLANETS FORM

Planets arise as a natural result of the star-formation process. Stars are born from large clouds of gas and dust. That gas and dust spin in space, flattening into a disk the way pizza dough does when a baker tosses it. The center of the disk becomes a star, whereas the rest of the disk may form planets.

Within the disk, bits of dust begin to clump together. Those clumps eventually get bigger and become rocky objects called protoplanets. Protoplanets smack into each other and stick together to make planets.

The asteroids in our solar system are leftover planetesimals, or small planets from the early solar system. Jupiter's gravity stirred them up and prevented them from sticking together. Astronomers also have found evidence of asteroids in other star systems.

If a rocky planet grows large enough, it can collect and hold on to surrounding hydrogen gas. That's how the gas giants of our outer solar system grew so big.

Follow the artwork below from top left to bottom right to see how a star and its planets form from a single disk of gas and dust. As the infant star gathers hydrogen gas, leftover rocky bits stick together like giant dust bunnies. Eventually, those cosmic clumps grow to become full-size planets. Here, a comet is streaking toward them.

Astronomers didn't discover planets outside our solar system until 1992. Then, three Earth-size planets were detected about 900 light-years away. Instead of orbiting a normal star, they were orbiting a dead star known as a pulsar.

In 1995, Swiss astronomers found the first planet orbiting a normal star. Named 51 Pegasi b, it has about half the mass of Jupiter; unlike Jupiter, it orbits very close to its star and has a year that is four days long.

Since the discovery of 51 Pegasi b, astronomers have confirmed more than 900 planets orbiting other stars. As well as "hot Jupiters," like 51 Pegasi b, they include such oddball characters as "puffy planets," as light as cork, and coal-black planets. Most discovered so far don't look like they would support Earthlike life. They are too hot or too cold, bathed in deadly radiation, or circle their suns in long loopy orbits. But a few are promising. Planet Kepler 22b, about 600 light-years away, is a large "super-Earth" that seems to be in the life-friendly habitable zone of its sunlike star.

Astronomers have even found a planet in our neighborhood. It circles Alpha Centauri, in the star system closest to Earth.

Recently astronomers discovered an Earth-size planet called Alpha Centauri B. It is orbiting a star that is very close to our own sun. Located only 4.3 light-years away, this planet is no twin of Earth. It appears to be a heat-blasted world covered with molten rock (art right).

1. Wobbling Star

Look for a star that wobbles when a planet's gravity tugs at it.

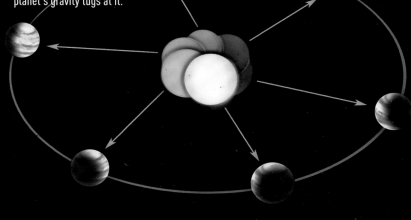

2. Eclipsing Star's Dimming Light

Look for a star that dims when a planet crosses in front of it.

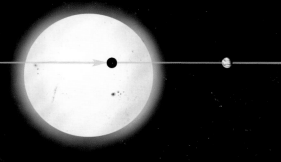

It's hard to find planets around other stars. The stars are very far away, and planets are so small and dim that seeing one next to a star is like trying to see a firefly sitting next to a spotlight. Only in the past decade have astronomers gained the tools they need to find alien worlds, such as the orbiting space telescopes Kepler, Spitzer, and CoRoT.

Since a star is much easier to see than a planet, astronomers usually hunt planets by looking for their effect on their host star. Most of the 900 known alien worlds were found by looking for wobbling stars.

Just as the star's gravity tugs on the planet, the planet's gravity tugs on the star. In this gravitational dance, the star wobbles back and forth.

If it wobbles toward and away from us, we can use a spectrograph (an instrument similar to a prism that splits the light of the star into a spectrum of colors) to look for a slight shift in the star's movement. That is the way 51 Pegasi b was found. We can j136 also look for stars that wobble left and right or up and down across the sky, but those searches are much harder because the wobble in the star's apparent position is so tiny.

Planet hunters have had great success by looking for planets that eclipse their stars, making the star's light dim ever so slightly. (Since we are so far away, the planet appears to cover only a fraction of the star's disk.) Eclipse searches can find smaller planets than the search for "wobblers"—even planets as small as Earth.

A few planets have been seen directly, using methods that block out or cancel out the glaring light of their suns. Astronomers are excited about direct imaging, because it may let them get a look at the planets' atmospheres.

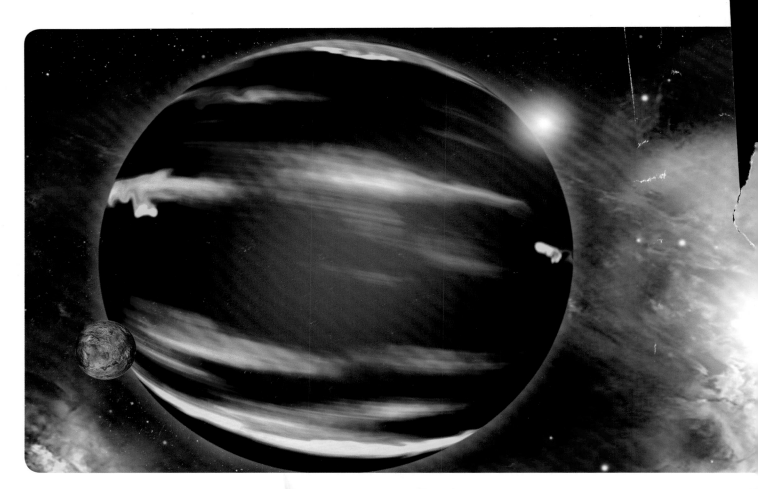

The distant planet HD 189733 b (art left), located 60 light-years from Earth, is covered by a dark layer of clouds that hides all its surface features, making it one of the blackest planets ever found in the universe.

The gas giant planet Epsilon Eridani b, seen from one of its moons in this artwork, orbits a star a little cooler than our sun. Since the planet is more than 300 million miles (483 million km) from its star, it and its moons would be too cold to support life.

The Milky Way and other large galaxies are home to a special kind of star cluster: a globular cluster. These round balls hold up to a million stars. They are spread over a volume of several tens to about 200 light-years in diameter. If you think of the sun as living in a quiet suburb, then the stars in a globular cluster are living in a crowded city center.

If you were to visit a planet inside a globular cluster, the night sky would be spectacular! From Earth we see only a few thousand stars with the unaided eye. The sky of a globular-cluster planet would be filled with a hundred thousand stars or more.

These clusters contain the oldest stars in our galaxy— almost as old as the universe itself. Many aging red giants and dead white dwarfs live in globular clusters.

Globular clusters orbit the center of the Milky Way in all directions, some looping high above or below our galaxy. Astronomer Harlow Shapley mapped globular clusters as a way to figure out the size and shape of our galaxy. He argued that since we see more globular clusters in one direction than in the other, we must be off to the side of the Milky Way.

This art shows the night sky as seen from a cave opening on a rocky planet orbiting a star in a globular cluster. Thousands of nearby stars would make clear nights much lighter than they are on Earth.

Since so many stars are packed so close together in globular clusters, they're very bright and visible across great distances of space. That makes them favorite targets for a lot of backyard astronomers. Through a large telescope, a globular cluster looks like a large ball of stars filling the eyepiece with a spectacular display.

In small telescopes, globular clusters look more like fuzzy cotton balls. In fact, they look a lot like comets, which is why Charles Messier's catalogue of objects lists a lot of globular clusters.

Globular clusters are so crowded that sometimes two stars will collide to form a more massive star that burns hot and blue, appearing younger than it really is. Since those stars look like they've aged more slowly, lagging behind their neighbors, astronomers have named them blue stragglers.

Omega Centauri (photo below) is the largest and brightest globular cluster in the Milky Way. It contains millions of stars in a sphere 150 light-years across. Omega Centauri is best viewed from locations near Earth's Equator.

Centaurus

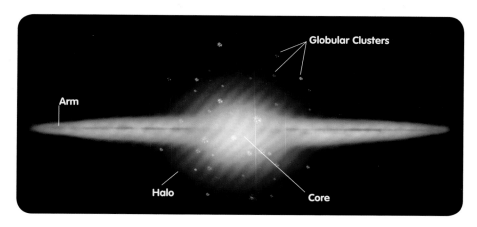

All spiral galaxies are surrounded by a halo of globular clusters (art left). The stars in the globular clusters were the first to form as the galaxy structures grew.

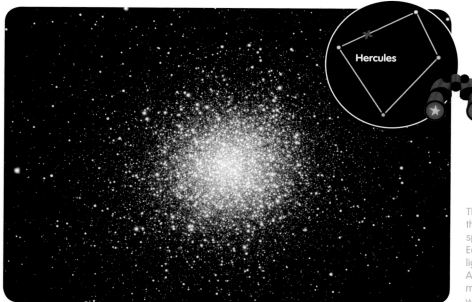

The Hercules Globular Cluster, or M13, in the Hercules constellation (photo left) offers a spectacular view to observers north of the Equator. M13 is bright even though it is 25,000 light-years away. In 1974, astronomers used the Arecibo radio telescope in Puerto Rico to send a message toward it. If aliens live there, they won't get the message for 25,000 years.

The globular cluster M2 (photo left) is compact, which makes it more easily visible in small backyard telescopes. It's located on the opposite side of the galactic center from Earth, more than 37,000 light-years away.

Billions of galaxies with hundreds of billions of stars populate our universe. Galaxies come in many varieties. Our home, the Milky Way, is a spiral galaxy. All spiral galaxies have a disk of stars. The stars gather into curlicues called spiral arms that extend from the galaxy's center to its edges. Some galaxies have tightly wound spiral arms; others have loosely wound spiral arms.

Some spiral galaxies are just a disk and are as flat as a pancake. Others, including the Milky Way, have a big, central ball of stars called a bulge. The bulge often contains older stars, whereas the flat disk holds younger stars.

A barred spiral galaxy has a central bar, or rectangular clump, of stars that lies across the middle of the galaxy. The spiral arms extend from the

The galactic zoo is shown in the art above. An elliptical galaxy has a distinctly orange-yellow color because it contains mostly old, redder stars. Unlike spiral galaxies, ellipticals like this one typically hold little or no dust.

A spiral galaxy has older stars in its central bulge and young, blue stars in its disk and spiral arms. Dark patches show where large clumps of interstellar dust block starlight.

This unusual galaxy is in between a spiral and an elliptical, sharing characteristics of both. It has the flattened shape of a spiral, but its yellowish color and lack of dust are more like an elliptical.

ends of the bar, instead of from the center of the galaxy. Astronomers think that a galactic bar might form when a galaxy is disturbed by the gravity of another galaxy that passes nearby, or even collides with it.

The Milky Way is a barred spiral, but from Earth we're looking almost directly at one end of the bar, so it's hard to see from our location.

Another common type of galaxy is the elliptical galaxy. Elliptical galaxies are all bulge and no disk. They can be round, football-shaped, or anything in between. They tend to be made up of only old stars.

Another type of galaxy has no definite shape. Because of that, it's called an irregular galaxy. The nearby Magellanic Clouds are irregular galaxies, and in the beginning of the universe, the first galaxies that formed were irregulars.

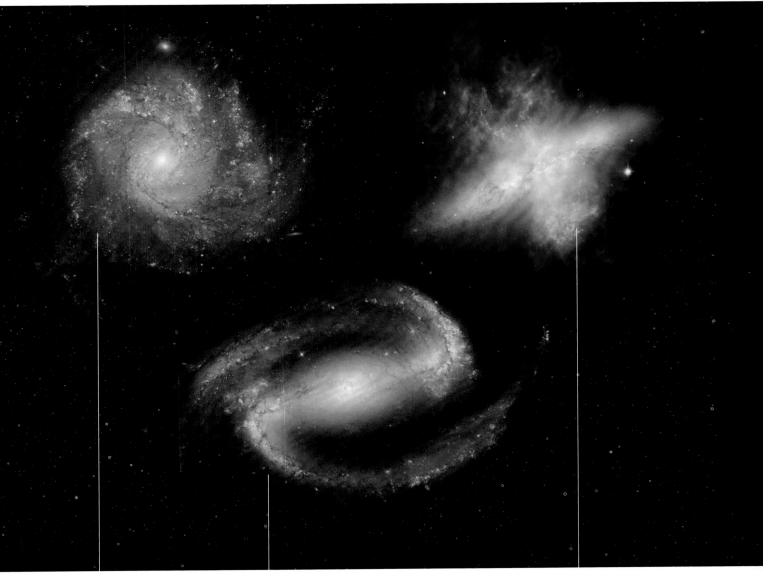

A face-on view is the best way to enjoy the dramatic sweep of a galaxy's spiral arms. This spiral has a very small bulge compared to its disk.

This barred spiral galaxy appears tightly wound up. Sometime in its past, another galaxy probably passed nearby, ripping away some of its stars and gases and spinning the rest into a flattened S shape.

Irregular galaxies don't have the well-defined shapes of spirals or ellipticals. In this composite photograph, green shows where stars are, while blue and red highlight hot gas ejected from the galaxy into intergalactic space.

The closest large galaxy to the Milky Way is the Andromeda galaxy, also called M31. Andromeda is like the Milky Way's big sister, since it's more than twice as large as our galaxy. The Milky Way is 100,000 light-years across and holds about 400 billion stars. By comparison, Andromeda is about 260,000 light-years across and holds a trillion stars.

Another close neighbor of the Milky Way is the Triangulum galaxy, or M33. M33 is the runt of the litter. It is only 50,000 light-years across, with about 100 billion stars. Unlike many galaxies, M33 has no giant black hole at its center.

Until the 1920s, astronomers thought M31 and M33 were nearby gaseous nebulas and part of the Milky Way. Then Edwin Hubble discovered that M31 and M33 are separate galaxies. Sometime in the future, the Milky Way and Andromeda will collide, temporarily forming one big galaxy called Milkomeda. Then, to complicate matters, M33 may collide with this large galaxy, creating an even larger one. We'll leave it up to future astronomers to name this new galaxy!

The Andromeda galaxy is visible to your unaided eye if you're in a dark location. This long-exposure photograph taken with a small telescope shows Andromeda's full glory.

Stars don't collide too often because they're very far apart, relative to their size. Galaxies are much closer to each other relative to their size, so they collide frequently. Galactic collisions were even more common in the past, when the universe was smaller and galaxies were closer together.

When galaxies collide, strange things can happen. Sometimes a small galaxy punches through the center of a larger galaxy, leaving a hole and a surrounding ring of stars and creating a ring galaxy. Sometimes a large galaxy consumes a small one, destroying all signs that the smaller one ever existed. If the giant black holes at the centers of two galaxies collide, the impact can send one of them flying through space like a monstrous billiard ball at millions of miles per hour.

Right now, the Milky Way is swallowing at least one "dwarf" galaxy. On the far side of the galactic center from Earth, the Sagittarius dwarf elliptical galaxy is plunging through the disk of the Milky Way. The Milky Way's stronger gravity is ripping apart the dwarf. Eventually its stars will become part of the Milky Way.

More than 200 million years ago, M32, a smaller galaxy, punched through the disk of Andromeda. Ripples of

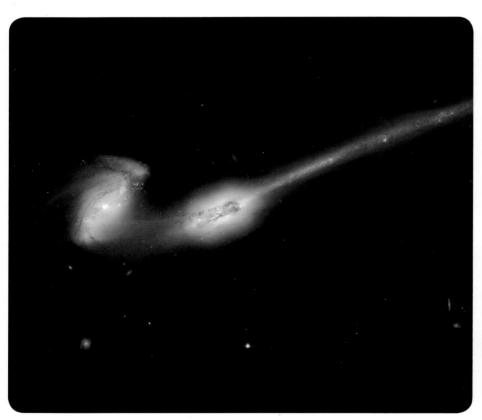

The Hubble Space Telescope captured this view of two galaxies playing a game of cat and mouse or, in this case, mouse and mouse. These colliding galaxies were nicknamed "the mice" because of the long tails of stars and gas thrown off them during the collision. They're located 300 million light-years from Earth.

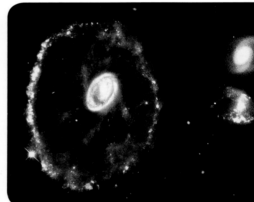

The Cartwheel Galaxy (photo top), 500 million light-years from Earth, suffered a head-on collision with another galaxy. Gravitational forces from the collision formed the two stunning rings of gas and newborn stars. The Whirlpool Galaxy (photo above) has a small companion known as NGC 5195. As the two galaxies brush past each other, gravity from NGC 5195 may be molding the dramatic spiral structure seen in the Whirlpool Galaxy.

interstellar dust spread out through Andromeda like water ripples in a pond. M32 survived the encounter, but one day it will be devoured by Andromeda.

When two galaxies close to the same size interact, the results are even more dramatic. Gravity can fling off streams of stars as the galaxies whip around each other. Gas clouds in the two galaxies may merge, fueling bursts of star formation.

In some colliding galaxies, stars form a hundred times faster than in calm galaxies like the Milky Way. Those stars live fast and die quickly. A star explodes as a supernova every couple of years there, compared to an average of once every hundred years in the Milky Way. Astronomers call colliding, starburst galaxies "supernova factories," since they produce supernovas so quickly.

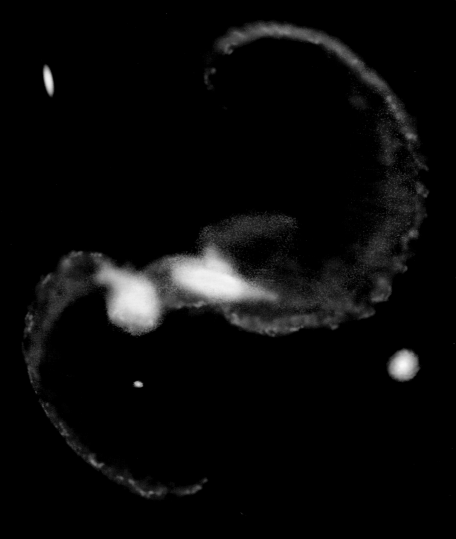

When galaxies collide, chaotic collisions and disruptions occur. One of the consequences is that planets can be ejected into space (photo above). Without a star to warm them, these orphaned planets now travel through space alone.

The Milky Way and Andromeda are on a collision course, approaching each other at a speed of about 300,000 miles (483,000 km) per hour. In a few billion years, these two galaxies will ram together (art above) to become a football-shaped, elliptical galaxy.

Since the Milky Way and Andromeda are both large, their collision will be particularly dramatic. The "damage" will be greater, just as the collision of two dump trucks would bend a lot more metal than if a small vehicle were to smack into a truck.

As the two galaxies interact gravitationally, some stars will be tossed outward, escaping into intergalactic space. Others will be flung from a galaxy's outskirts into the core (art above). Stars that once orbited in an orderly disk may be sent into new orbits that zoom outward before plunging back down, looping around and out again.

By the time the Milky Way and Andromeda collide, our star, the sun, will be no more than a white dwarf.

Both the Milky Way and Andromeda hold plenty of gas that could form new stars. Most likely, a burst of star formation will take place when the collision happens. Thousands of new stars and planetary systems will be born. Older stars will be lost, ejected from both galaxies. Many new stars will quickly die off and explode as supernovas. The new galaxy will be an energetic place for millions of years after the collision.

The twin Magellanic Clouds, or Clouds of Magellan, are not really clouds at all. They're galaxies visible deep in the southern half of the sky. North of the Equator you can't see them. Because of this, they remained unknown to most of the Western world until the voyage of Ferdinand Magellan.

In 1519, he sailed from Spain with a crew of about 270 men, hoping to travel around the world. Magellan died along the way, but 18 members of his crew returned safely in 1522. With them, they brought their observations of the southern sky. When European astronomers used the mariners' records to make sky charts, they named two objects after Magellan, calling those objects the Large and Small Magellanic Clouds.

ABOUT THE CLOUDS

Although they may look like glowing clouds fixed to the sky, the Magellanic Clouds are both irregular galaxies that have been twisted and warped by the Milky Way's gravity.

Astronomers used to think that the Magellanic Clouds were permanent companions of the Milky Way, orbiting around our galaxy. Now scientists think these travelers may be "just passing through."

The Large Magellanic Cloud is located about 160,000 light-years from Earth. It's about

one-twentieth as large as our galaxy in diameter and holds about one-tenth as many stars. The Small Magellanic Cloud is located about 200,000 light-years from Earth. It's about ten times smaller than its companion and a hundred times smaller than the Milky Way.

SUPERNOVA 1987A

In February 1987, astronomers spotted an exploding star in the Large Magellanic Cloud. Since it was the first supernova observed that year, it was named Supernova 1987A. This was the closest supernova to Earth seen since the invention of the telescope.

At its brightest, Supernova 1987A shone with the energy of a billion suns and could be seen with the unaided eye, despite how far away it was. It slowly faded over time and now is visible only with a telescope.

Debris from Supernova 1987A formed a supernova remnant. Astronomers have searched the remnant looking for a neutron star that might have been created by the explosion, but they haven't found it. The explosion may have created a black hole instead.

When Magellan sailed into the Southern Hemisphere, his crew spotted two objects (top right in art) that no European had seen before. He used them as markers to navigate, not realizing they were actually companions to the Milky Way (middle, reflected on the sea).

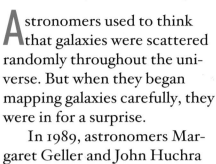

Astronomers used to think that galaxies were scattered randomly throughout the universe. But when they began mapping galaxies carefully, they were in for a surprise.

In 1989, astronomers Margaret Geller and John Huchra announced that, rather than being random, galaxies are clustered into gigantic structures. Dozens of galaxies they measured were lined up at about the same distance, forming a "great wall." Scientists have found many more walls of galaxies since then.

The universe started out very smooth, with matter spread out almost evenly through space. Over the past 13.8 billion years, gravity has pulled that matter together. Now, the universe close to us is very clumpy.

The Milky Way is part of a galaxy cluster called the Local Group. The Andromeda spiral galaxy, M33, the Magellanic Clouds, and about 30 dwarf galaxies all currently belong to the Local Group. The Milky Way and Andromeda are two of its largest members.

Illuminated in the background by glowing strings of primordial galaxies, most modern galaxies cluster into huge cosmic walls (art left) pulled together by their mutual gravity. More-distant galaxies are redder in color, a fact that helps astronomers measure distances across the visible universe.

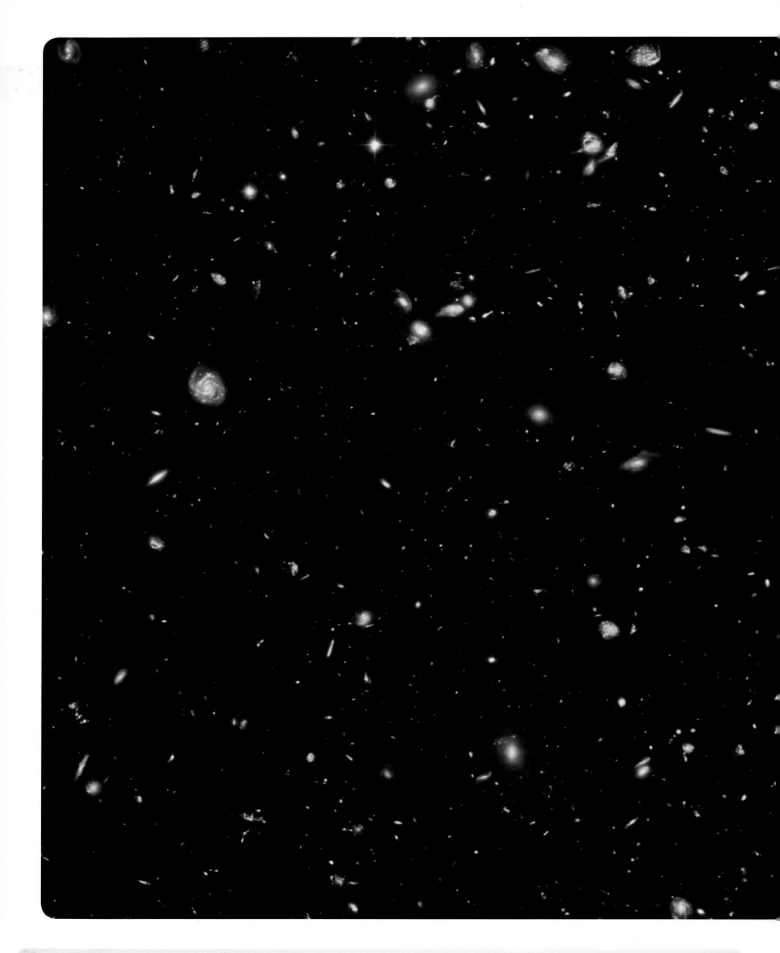

In 2004, astronomers unveiled the longest time-length photograph of the sky ever made. The Hubble Ultra Deep Field shows an area (field) of the sky one-fiftieth the size of the full moon, or smaller than a grain of sand held at arm's length. It required a total exposure time of a million seconds, or 11.3 days, and it reveals objects ten billion times fainter than what can be seen with the human eye.

"Deep" refers to areas of space outside our solar system. Some galaxies in this photograph are very faint because they're almost 13 billion light-years away. That means we're seeing them 13 billion years ago, when the universe was young.

The Hubble Ultra Deep Field shows about 10,000 galaxies. Some are spirals and ellipticals similar to nearby galaxies, but many others are oddballs—galactic toddlers still growing and developing.

The Ultra Deep Field will remain our best view of the early universe until Hubble's successor, the James Webb Space Telescope, is launched in 2018.

Eight hundred photos taken over four months by the Hubble Space Telescope (just above) were processed and assembled to make this stunning view (left). It encompasses 10,000 galaxies, each containing about 200 billion stars.

Seeing the light of very distant galaxies is a great achievement for astronomers. But they face an even more difficult problem: seeing the dark.

Scientists have known since the 1930s that the universe has unseen matter whose gravity pulls on visible matter. No one knows, however, what this dark matter really is. Trying to solve this puzzle is one of the most important problems in modern astronomy.

Some scientists think this mysterious stuff might be made of heavy, dark chunks of matter, such as lightless brown dwarf stars. These kinds of objects are called MACHOs (MAssive Compact Halo Objects). But most scientists think that dark matter probably consists of huge numbers of tiny subatomic particles, known as WIMPs (Weakly Interacting Massive Particles).

They are hunting for these particles using large, sophisticated detectors. For now, though, the true nature of dark matter is a mystery.

Astronomers did find hints of dark matter when they studied rotating spiral galaxies, including the Milky Way. Rotating galaxies are like merry-go-rounds. Their speed depends on on how much weight is on them and where it is located, whether in the middle or on the edges.

All of the galaxies astronomers examined were rotating faster than expected—so fast that they should fly apart, scattering stars like riders who aren't holding on to the handles. Strong gravity had to be holding the galaxies together. That gravity came from unseen dark matter.

There are many other clues that dark matter exists. For one, galaxy clusters hold hot intergalactic gas. The gas is so hot that it should escape like steam from a teapot. The gravity of dark matter holds onto it.

In 2006, scientists got the strongest evidence yet that dark matter is real. They studied a pair of colliding galaxies and found that gas and stars were clustered in one spot, while the strongest gravity was concentrated in a different spot. The collision had dragged visible matter and dark matter in opposite directions.

Even the clumpiness of the universe shows that dark matter exists. Without the extra gravity of dark matter, visible matter wouldn't have had time to pull itself together to form galaxies and galaxy clusters. In that sense, we owe our very existence to something we've never seen.

We thought we knew what the universe was, but we don't. Almost five-sixths of all matter is unseen and unknown. Astronomers hope to find the door (symbolized in the art left) that opens onto the answer to the mystery of dark matter.

To understand the accelerating universe, you first have to understand the birth of the universe—the big bang. This was not an explosion that tossed a bunch of atoms and energy into empty space. The big bang was an explosion of space itself. It created space where none existed before. And space is still being created right now.

When we say the universe is expanding, we mean that space itself is expanding. Galaxies rush away from each other not because they are speeding through space, but because the space between them is growing. A galaxy is like a person standing on a moving walkway. The person moves because the walkway moves.

SURPRISE!

Astronomers thought that the expansion of the universe had been slowing ever since the big bang. The pull of gravity from all the matter in the universe, both normal matter and dark matter, should see to that. The only debate was whether the universe would slow to a stop and reverse, collapsing into a "big crunch," or whether the universe would just keep slowing down without ever really stopping.

In 1998, astronomers got a big surprise. Two teams studying distant supernovas found that those star explosions were dimmer than expected. Since light grows dimmer the farther away the light source is, the supernovas were more distant than expected. So the universe must be expanding faster than scientists had expected.

DARK ENERGY

In fact, calculations showed that the universe wasn't just growing faster than we thought; it was actually speeding up. Something must be providing a cosmic push. Astronomers named that mysterious something dark energy. The reverse of gravity, dark energy is pushing things away from each other.

No one knows what dark energy is, but many scientists are trying to answer that question. So far, it seems that dark energy is a property of space itself. The more space grows due to cosmic expansion, the more dark energy grows, and the more "push" there is to speed up the universe.

Whatever dark energy may be, its influence will decide the fate of our universe.

A mysterious force that astronomers call dark energy is speeding up the expansion of the universe. Galaxies are flying away from each other faster and faster (art right).

We are on a one-way trip. Since the universe is expanding, everything is getting farther and farther apart. At some point, even our closest neighbors will have moved on. Before that happens, however, the Milky Way and Andromeda will collide. In a few billion years, they'll form a new combined galaxy that will pull in all the smaller galaxies in our neighborhood and swallow them up. More-distant galaxies will escape and move beyond our sight, leaving only one visible galaxy: our own.

Astronomers think our galaxy, and our universe, may end in one of two ways. In the "Big Chill" version, the universe will suffer a slow and steady decline. Stars and gases will drift apart and cool down. No new stars will be born. Stars that already exist will live their

lives and burn out. Many trillions of years from now, all that will be left is a galaxy of black holes, neutron stars, and cold, black dwarfs that gradually fade away.

In the "Big Rip" version, the universe will expand faster and faster over time. Planets, stars, and galaxies will be violently torn apart, right down to their atoms.

Which version turns out to be correct depends on what we learn about dark energy. When we find out what it is, and whether it will always be in effect, we will know whether the universe will end with a sigh or a bang.

Tens of billions of years in the future, stars like our sun will have died. In this "Big Chill" scenario, only faint, red stars that live for a long time will remain. Those fading embers will shed little warmth on worlds grown cold and quiet (art below).

OTHER UNIVERSES

When astronomers speak of the universe, they mean the observable universe—everything that we can see or detect with instruments. But what if there is more out there that we can't observe?

Astronomers have several ideas about how our universe formed. Some believe that a universe can pop into existence from a black hole (art below). If that's true, there could be thousands of other universes that we can't detect.

Using mathematics, scientists not only can imagine but also can describe in detail other possible universes, with different laws of physics. This is more than idle speculation. Other universes may actually exist.

To understand this mind-bending idea, consider what the word "dimension" means. In our everyday experience, a dimension is a direction in space. We live in a three-dimensional world—we can move forward and backward, left and right, up and down.

Physicist Albert Einstein showed that time also is a dimension, linked permanently to the other three. Past-future is the fourth dimension. So physicists have described the fabric of the cosmos as being four-dimensional space-time.

The most recent theory for the birth of our universe suggests that colliding branes (art above) may be the power source behind the big bang. If such collisions happen over and over, then universes may have been formed and re-formed many times in the past.

A FIFTH DIMENSION?

Recently, physicists have begun to think there may be more than the four familiar dimensions. The true nature of everything may involve many dimensions, but we can't perceive other dimensions with our senses.

We're like ants crawling on the surface of a giant hot-air balloon. The ants perceive only the flat, two-dimensional fabric stretching off in all directions as far as they can see. We perceive four-dimensional space-time stretching in all directions, when actually other dimensions may exist.

Scientists speculate that the visible universe may be a four-dimensional membrane, or brane for short, moving through unseen dimensions. Other branes, or parallel universes, may also exist. We would never be able to communicate with these other universes, much less travel among them.

COLLIDING BRANES

New research suggests that the event we call the big bang actually occurred when our brane collided with a neighboring brane. The collision generated the heat energy and push of expansion that we call the big bang. A lot of work lies ahead to determine if the colliding-brane theory is true.

In this imagined, alien world, creatures don't see the colors that we do. Instead, they detect infrared heat like an infrared camera does.

Earth is the perfect world for life. But what makes it so special? Actually, there are a number of things.

To begin with, Earth is in the right orbit circling the sun. Not too hot and not too cold, it has just the right temperature range to support life and keep the water in our oceans from freezing or boiling.

Next, we orbit the right kind of star. Some stars have much shorter lifetimes than ours, leaving little time for life to evolve on the planets orbiting them. Some stars send out lethal amounts of radiation, which fry the surrounding planets and their moons. Our sun is a long-lived, stable star— perfect for supporting life.

Earth is also the right size. It's large enough to generate the gravity needed to hold an atmosphere and not let it float away. We have a stabilizing moon as well, and a tilted axis that moderates weather cycles.

Finally, Earth is located out in an arm of the Milky Way where there aren't devastating explosions. All of these things put together mean we live on a perfect world.

Light from the sun (peeking over the edge of Earth in the art) gives Earth just the right temperatures for life. The moon helps stabilize its rotation. Jupiter protects us from asteroids; its gravity pulls them in before they reach us.

WHAT IS LIFE?

This seems like such an easy question to answer. Everybody knows singing birds are alive and rocks are not. When we start studying plants, bacteria, and other odd microscopic creatures, though, things get more complicated. So what exactly is life?

Most scientists agree that if something can move on its own, reproduces to make more copies of itself, grows in size to become more complex in structure over time, takes in nutrients to survive, gives off waste products, and responds to external stimuli such as increased sunlight and changes in temperature, it's alive!

Biologists classify living organisms by how they get their energy. Algae, green plants, and some bacteria use sunlight as an energy source. Human beings, fungi, and some archaea use chemicals to provide energy. When we eat food, chemicals in our digestive system turn the food into fuel.

Living things inhabit land, sea, and air. Life also thrives deep beneath the oceans and embedded in rocks miles below the Earth's crust, in ice, and in other extreme environments. The life-forms that thrive in these environments are called extremophiles. Some of these draw directly upon the chemicals surrounding them for energy. Since these are very different forms of life than what we're used to, we may not think of them as alive, but they are. If there is life on Mars, Titan, or somewhere else in the solar system, it could be like these extremophiles, and if we find it, we want to be sure to recognize it as life.

To understand how a living

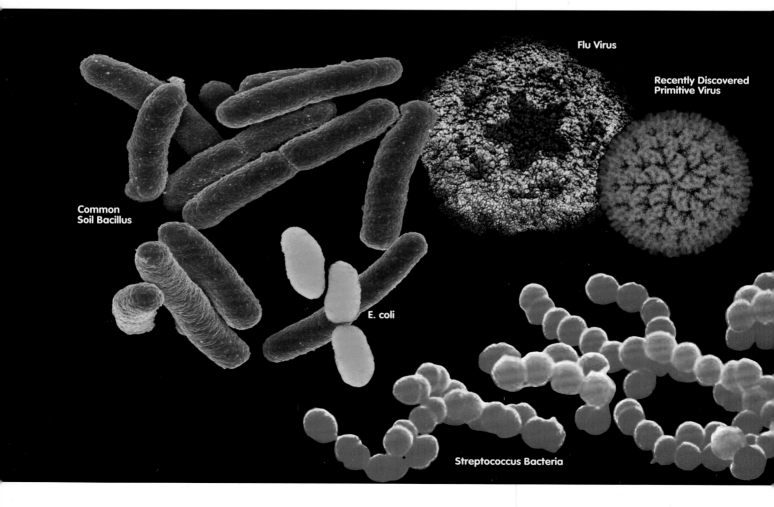

Common Soil Bacillus

E. coli

Flu Virus

Recently Discovered Primitive Virus

Streptococcus Bacteria

organism works, it helps to look at one example of its simplest form—the single-cell bacteria called streptococcus. There are many kinds of these tiny organisms, and some are responsible for human illnesses. What makes us sick or uncomfortable are the waste products the bacteria give off in our bodies.

A single streptococcus bacterium is so small that at least 500 of them could fit on the dot above this letter "i." Under a microscope, magnified to a thousand times their true size, they look like little round water balloons joined in long strings. Like a water balloon, they have an outside covering. Sort of like the skin on our bodies, this cell membrane separates the outside world from the inside, working parts of the j162 bacterium. Inside the membrane, thousands of molecules in different shapes and structures float in a gel.

These bacteria are one of the simplest forms of life we know. They have no moving parts, no lungs, no brain, no heart, no liver, no leaves or fruit. And yet, this life-form reproduces and makes more of itself, grows in size by producing long chain structures, takes in nutrients, and gives off toxins. That's why your body runs a temperature when it detects a strep infection. It's defending itself from an invader!

How did a random collection of nonliving molecules come together, get organized, and become alive? We're not sure, but these are questions scientists are trying to answer.

Scientists think life began on Earth some 4.1 to 3.9 billion years ago, but no fossils exist from that time. The earliest fossils ever found are from the primitive life that existed 3.6 billion years ago. Other life-forms soon followed, and some of these are shown in the images below. Scientists continue to study how life evolved on Earth and whether or not it is possible that life exists on other planets.

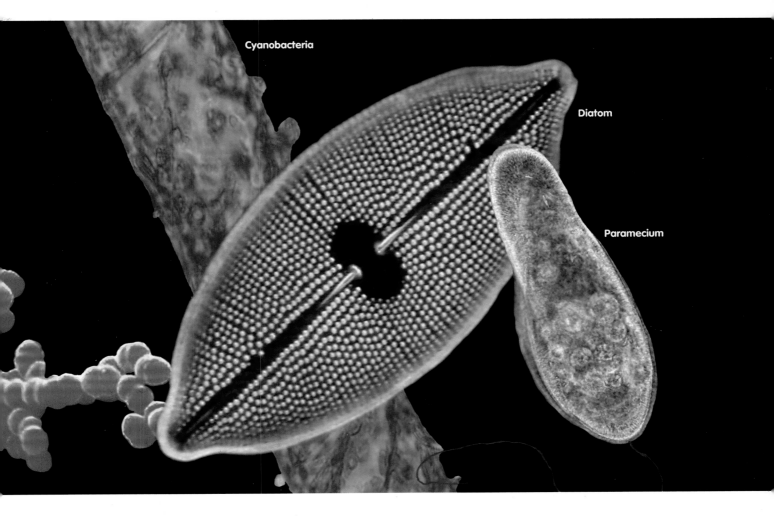

Cyanobacteria

Diatom

Paramecium

In 1976, when a Viking lander set down on the surface of Mars, no Martians were there to greet it. In one moment, the hope of finding intelligent life on Mars vanished. Now, more than 35 years later, no traces of life, not even microbes, have been discovered on Mars. The planet appears to be a vast desert wasteland. The surface water it used to have is locked up in the frozen polar ice caps. Life-supporting liquid water doesn't exist on the surface anymore. However, the Curiosity Rover is investigating an area of the planet to find out if conditions were once suitable for microbial life.

On Venus, life might have existed billions of years ago, but today the planet's extreme atmospheric pressure and heat would crush or cook life.

A few scientists still hold out hope that alien forms of life may be found bobbing along like cosmic jellyfish in the upper cloud layers of Venus or Jupiter, but this is very unlikely. So where do we search for life elsewhere in our solar system? The answer is four distant moons—one circling Jupiter and three orbiting Saturn.

Jupiter's moon Europa has dark, salty oceans under a thick shell of ice. A lake on the moon has also been discovered. Studies have hinted that other moons could also carry liquid water, and maybe even life.

There are three conditions on Europa, though, that may bump it off the list for harboring life. First, its oceans are not just dark—they're pitch black. No sunlight penetrates through the ice. Life could form without sunlight, but it would be much more difficult for that to happen.

Second, the water is too acid to support life. Third, Europa is bathed in lethal radiation emitted by Jupiter. Anything on or near the surface of Europa's icy world would be killed. If there is life on this moon, it will surely be small and very hardy. And if there are warm, hydrothermal vents on the ocean floor, it will probably be living in the thick ooze next to them.

Saturn's moon Titan may be another place to look for life in our solar system. There's a good chance Titan's methane-rich atmosphere may be the result of primitive living organisms. Underneath its frozen methane lakes, there may be layers of liquid ammonia. Even though it's poisonous to life on our planet today, ammonia wasn't harmful to the first life-forms on Earth. So if there is life on Titan, it could be similar to early life on Earth, but not like any kind of life here now.

Scientists have also discovered that Saturn's moon Dione has a thin layer of oxygen in its atmosphere and another of its moons, Enceladus, contains liquid water.

On Saturn's moon Titan there are whole lakes of liquid methane. In this image of Titan's surface, taken on the Cassini flyby mission in 2006, the lakes look lavender, but that's because the color has been changed in the photograph.

After drilling through almost half a mile of ice, a futuristic hydrobot (art above) probes Europa's dark waters. Surface temperatures are frigid here, but the gravitational pull of Jupiter and possible volcanic activity on the ocean floor may keep the deeper water from freezing.

The possibility that intelligent beings exist out there on other worlds is something humans have imagined for a long, long time. Though there may be some forms of life on Jupiter's or Saturn's moons, there's probably no other intelligent life in the solar system.

To find intelligent life, we have to look elsewhere. Astronomers have discovered about 900 planets circling nearby stars. Most are giant worlds, either very hot or very cold.

Scientists are pretty certain we won't find intelligent life on these worlds. However, they also believe that we will soon begin to find more small, Earth-like planets.

There are two theories about the source of intelligent life beyond Earth. Many scientists believe intelligent life is a natural part of evolution and is common throughout the universe.

Another group believes intelligent life is rare and begins in one place, then spreads to other worlds. In other words, one species ends up colonizing many other worlds.

For more than 50 years, organizations have been listening for radio messages sent by other intelligent civilizations. So far, no ETs have left a text message or return address. But there are billions of cosmic bodies out there to try and listen to. NASA hopes to narrow the list of those bodies in the next few years.

In 2009, NASA launched the Kepler Mission. The spacecraft's telescope studies more than 100,000 stars in our galaxy, identifying those with potential Earth-like planets circling them. Kepler and ground-based telescopes have so far discovered seven planets that are near-Earth size and in the habitable zone of their star. In the next ten years, we could find our first intelligent, alien civilization.

On this imagined distant world (art right), alien technology is advanced and similar to our own. But the aliens, shown in the foreground, don't resemble us at all.

THE DRAKE EQUATION

$$N = R^* \times f_p \times n_e \times f_l \times f_i \times f_c \times L$$

More than 50 years ago, astronomer Frank Drake came up with this equation to figure out how many intelligent civilizations might exist in our galaxy. He considered the possible number of civilizations that might be capable of communicating, the fraction of stars with planets, average number of planets and how many could support life, how many would have intelligent beings who wanted to communicate, and how long those civilizations might last. Based on his assumptions and today's knowledge, there could be a few thousand alien civilizations somewhere out there among the hundreds of billions of stars in our galaxy.

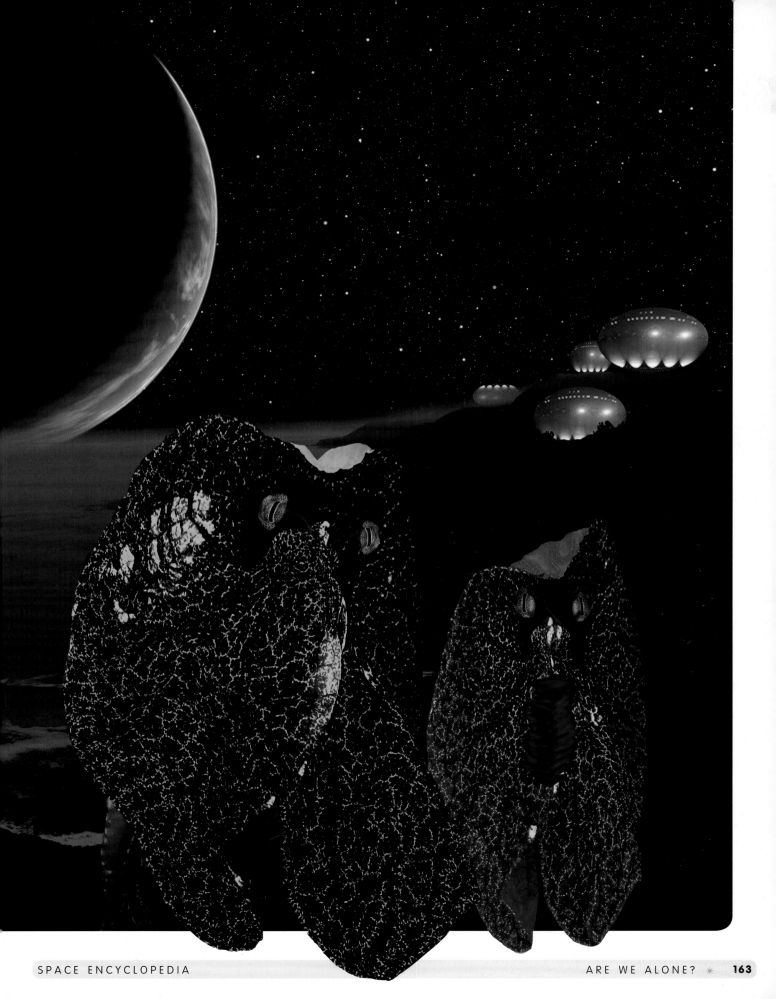

The aliens in Hollywood are created so people will buy movie tickets, not to be examples of the weirdness of biology. What really lives out there may be beyond anything we can imagine, let alone deal with. There could be two-foot-long green garden slugs that communicate using odors and see only in x-ray wavelengths of light. There have been some rather strange creatures here on our own world, too. If Earth hadn't had a run-in with an asteroid 65 million years ago, there might be some even stranger ones walking around today—and we wouldn't be one of them.

Before the asteroid hit, there was an Earth creature with two arms, two legs, and a head with two eyes. It stood upright and was about 6.5 feet (2 m) tall. Its name was *Troodon formosus*, and it was a dinosaur. After the asteroid hit and the climate changed, this

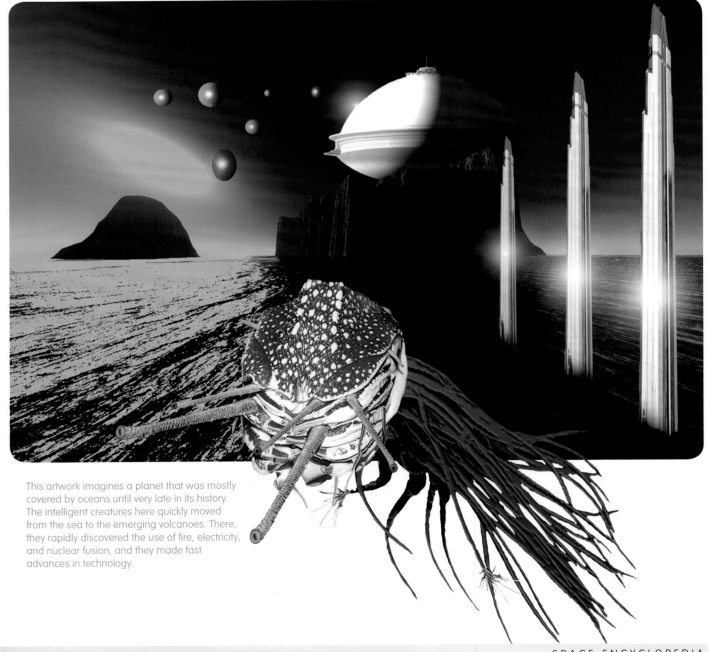

This artwork imagines a planet that was mostly covered by oceans until very late in its history. The intelligent creatures here quickly moved from the sea to the emerging volcanoes. There, they rapidly discovered the use of fire, electricity, and nuclear fusion, and they made fast advances in technology.

contender was knocked out of the race. Earth didn't become a planet of Dinopeople.

On other worlds, alien senses and anatomies may be so different that we won't even begin to be able to relate to them. They certainly won't look and talk like the aliens on *Star Trek.* If there were just slight changes in some of the physical conditions we take for granted here on Earth, life might follow some very odd pathways. If a planet had less gravity than Earth, life might grow taller and thinner. On a high-gravity world, body shapes might be shorter and more muscular. On a world with a thinner atmosphere, lungs might be larger and ears much bigger to pick up faint sounds. On freezing worlds or ocean planets, new shapes and adaptations would certainly appear. And what about life that looks nothing like anything we've ever seen? The creatures imagined in Hollywood may not look nearly as strange as the ones designed by nature.

This hot, humid imaginary world (art above) is a little too near its own sun. Its odd creatures stand almost nine feet (2.7 m) tall and move slowly away when approached. The upper, baggy part of their bodies is filled with helium, like a party balloon. They pose no threat to visitors, and they seem to communicate by using electrical impulses.

In the future, small supply ships and spaceships made from hollowed-out asteroids could service space stations.

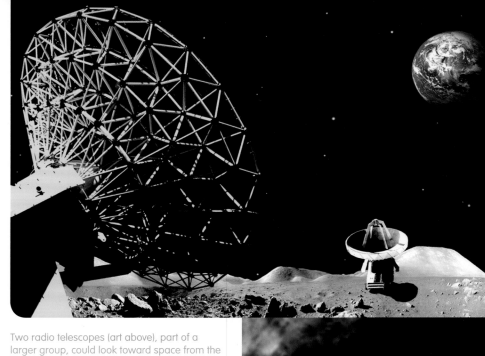

Our close neighbors in space—the moon and nearby asteroids—could give us new resources and new homes for our engineering projects. These resources will help us continue our exploration of the stars. Here are a few ways we might use the moon and asteroids in the future.

A TELESCOPE ON THE MOON

Airless, cold, and dead quiet, the moon is not a garden spot. It could be the ideal place for gazing into space, however. Radio telescopes could be placed there first, to capture radio waves from distant stars and planets. Placing the telescopes on the far side of the moon would shield them from interfering radio waves from Earth.

Next to be built might be a liquid mirror telescope (LMT). The light-collecting surface of an LMT is usually made of the shiny liquid metal mercury. Astronomers say that an LMT could be built at either of the moon's poles. Since the moon has no air, clouds, or city lights to get in the way, an LMT there might allow us to see farther than ever before.

ASTEROID TREASURES

As people begin to colonize the inner solar system, they'll need to build homes and labs, space stations and hotels. The raw

Two radio telescopes (art above), part of a larger group, could look toward space from the moon's surface. These telescopes would pick up radio waves, not visible light, from all kinds of objects: stars, nebulas, galaxies, even planets. Signals picked up by a group of telescopes can be combined into one big image.

Asteroid miners, both humans and robots, could carry metals and ice from an asteroid to a space freighter (art right). Scientists on the spacecraft would break down the ice into oxygen and hydrogen for fuel, and the asteroid's metal would be flown where it was needed.

materials for these buildings may well come from asteroids. Thousands of these chunks of rock, ice, and metal orbit close to Earth. Many are rich in iron and nickel; some contain platinum and gold. The ice in asteroids could be used for water, oxygen, and rocket fuel.

Asteroid miners could be humans or robots. They would dig the metal and ice out of the asteroid and ship it out on space freighters.

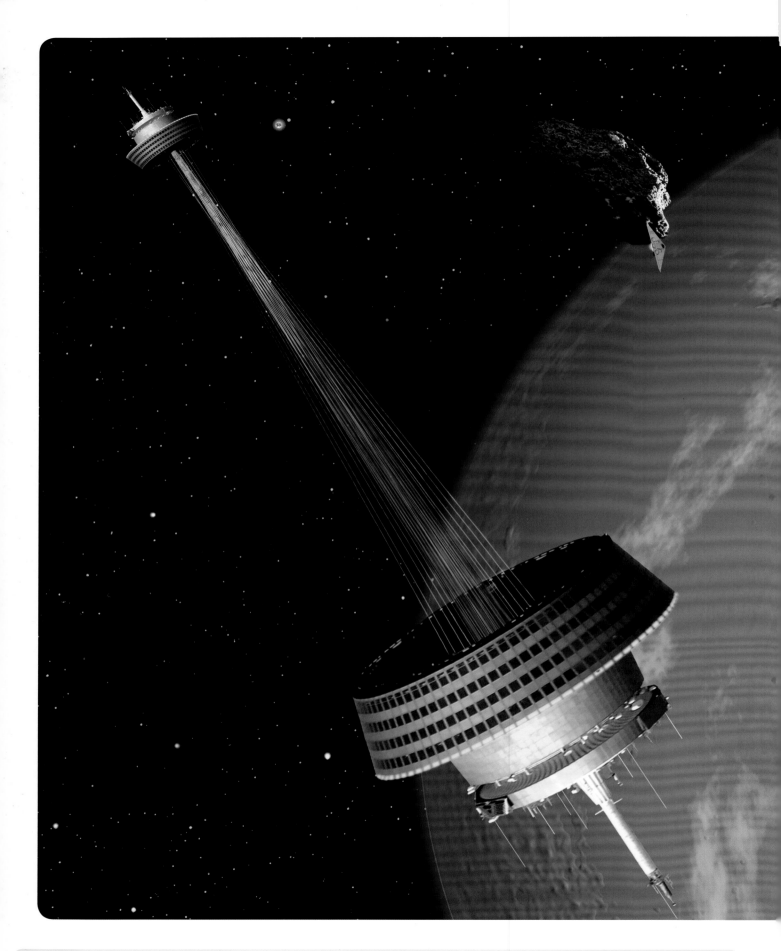

The space taxi is waiting. Mars-bound astronauts climb into the little craft, buckle up, and lift off from Earth. Soon they see their next stop: a huge spaceship soaring past in the dark. Their pilot pulls alongside, carefully bringing the taxi's speed to 13,000 miles (21,000 km) per hour to match the big craft's. With a few more delicate maneuvers, the pilot docks the taxi, and the astronauts enter their new home away from home: the moving Mars hotel.

Traveling to Mars on a regular spacecraft has some serious problems: The journey would require a huge amount of expensive fuel, and being weightless for a long time can badly weaken human bones and muscles. But "space hotels," also called cyclers, that ride the solar system's gravitational forces in a never ending loop between Mars and Earth wouldn't require much fuel, and each one would spin to create a kind of artificial gravity for the travelers inside. Cycler hotels could be the healthiest, cheapest, and most comfortable way to visit our planetary neighbor.

Although it's not luxurious, this imagined space hotel (far left in art) has comfortable little cabins, exercise machines, and games to play. After six months aboard, travelers would see the red planet looming in the hotel's windows. A space taxi would take the astronauts to the Martian surface to start their work.

Mars is a frigid desert with thin, poisonous air. But some scientists believe the planet could be transformed into a warm, green, Earthlike home by "terraforming" it.

Terraforming means to change something to make it like Earth. Terraforming Mars would be a huge project, taking hundreds or even thousands of years. The first step would be to make the Martian atmosphere warmer and thicker. This might be done by putting huge mirrors in orbit around the planet. The mirrors would focus the sun's rays on Mars's south pole and turn the carbon dioxide trapped in the polar ice into gas. Once in the atmosphere, the carbon dioxide would help hold heat next to the planet's surface.

This warmer atmosphere would melt the water ice now frozen in the soil, creating oceans and rivers. Then green plants could be grown to take in carbon dioxide and give off oxygen, which humans need to breathe. It would take thousands of years, but one day, people might be able to stroll around on Mars among green trees rustling in the wind.

1. Mars today (photo right): A cold and rocky desert, the red planet can't support human life. Its red tint comes from the iron in its soil. The planet chills under an average temperature of -80°F (-62°C). The atmosphere is 95 percent carbon dioxide and 100 times thinner than Earth's.

3. A green Mars: Under a thicker, warmer atmosphere fed by green plants, ice at Mars's poles and under the planet's surface would melt. Rivers would flow again on the surface and fill in ancient basins, creating oceans (art right).

2. Mars begins to green (art left): After creating a thicker atmosphere by melting ice from Mars's poles, scientists could bring in specially engineered plants from Earth. Grown in the warmest regions of Mars, the plants would take in carbon dioxide and give off breathable oxygen.

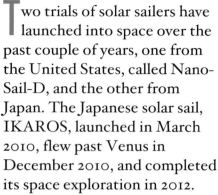

Two trials of solar sailers have launched into space over the past couple of years, one from the United States, called Nano-Sail-D, and the other from Japan. The Japanese solar sail, IKAROS, launched in March 2010, flew past Venus in December 2010, and completed its space exploration in 2012.

The idea behind solar sailing is pretty simple. Light is made of extremely tiny particles called photons. When photons bounce off objects, they push on those objects just a little bit. On Earth we don't notice this because other forces, like friction in the air, are so much stronger. But in space, where there is no air to get in the way, the gentle pressure of photons from the sun is enough to move a lightweight object.

Sunlight bouncing off a solar sail moves it—and the spacecraft attached to it—very slowly at first. Over time, the solar sailer picks up speed, moving faster and faster. By the time the sailer passes the outer planets, it can be traveling at 200,000 miles (324,000 km) per hour, ten times as fast as the space shuttle.

Solar sails can be made of shiny metallic cloth thinner than a butterfly's wing. They are also large. The U.S. solar sail NanoSail-D is one-fourth the size of a football field.

Human exploration will not be limited to our solar system. Now that we know that planets are common around other stars, we will have to visit them. And where better to start than with our closest neighbor, Alpha Centauri?

The Alpha Centauri star system has three stars. The two brightest, Alpha Centauri A and Alpha Centauri B, circle each other closely. A third star, Alpha Centauri C, is a red dwarf and orbits farther away. In 2012, tiny wobbles in the motion of Alpha Centauri B told astronomers that an Earth-size planet is orbiting it. The planet is too close to the sunlike star to support life. In fact, its surface is probably molten, like lava. But planets this size often have siblings, and many astronomers believe they will find other planets in more distant orbits.

The star's habitable zone starts about 65 million miles (105 million km) out. What will we find there? A bright blue and green world, like our own Earth? New forms of life? When we look at the planets of Alpha Centauri B, what will look back at us?

After a journey lasting nearly thirty years, the starship Columbus, launched by the inhabitants of Earth, 4.3 light-years away, arrives at the blue-green ringed world Terra II orbiting the orange star Alpha Centauri B. Terra II is the first planet to be explored for life beyond our own solar system.

IF THE AGE OF THE SOLAR SYSTEM WERE COMPARED TO THE LENGTH OF TIME IN A YEAR, HERE'S HOW LONG THINGS WOULD TAKE TO FORM AND DEVELOP.

JANUARY 1
On New Year's Day, the solar system begins condensing out of a swirling cloud of stardust.

JANUARY 7
The nuclear fires of our sun ignite.

JANUARY 28
A truly memorable day— Earth forms.

FEBRUARY
Through the month of February, Earth continues to shrink and cool.

MARCH 10
Escaped water vapor returns to Earth as rain, and oceans form.

APRIL 15
Somewhere within Earth's warm blue-green waters life begins.

MAY 22
Oxygen starts to form in the atmosphere.

JULY TO AUGUST
Life continues to develop.

SEPTEMBER 14
Somewhere in the oceanic depths, single-cell plants begin sexual reproduction.

OCTOBER
Multicell creatures and plants burst onto the scene.

DECEMBER 2
Some animals and plants begin to live on land.

DECEMBER 13
Dinosaurs appear.

DECEMBER 25
Dinosaurs disappear.

DECEMBER 31
At 5:00 in the evening, "Lucy," the oldest recognizable ancestor of the human tree, is born in Africa.

THE AMOUNT OF TIME WE HUMANS HAVE BEEN ON EARTH RELATIVE TO THE AGE OF THE SOLAR SYSTEM IS SO BRIEF THAT WE HAVE TO SWITCH NOW TO A STOPWATCH.

52 SECONDS BEFORE MIDNIGHT
On the last day of the year, Cro-Magnon humans, anatomically like modern humans, appear in Europe. Their cave paintings indicate they have an appreciation of culture.

40 SECONDS BEFORE MIDNIGHT
The pyramids are built.

33 SECONDS BEFORE MIDNIGHT
A succession of tribal peoples in what is now Britain assembles Stonehenge.

23 SECONDS BEFORE MIDNIGHT
The golden age of Greece is celebrated.

17 SECONDS BEFORE MIDNIGHT
Jesus is born in Bethlehem.

8 SECONDS BEFORE MIDNIGHT
The Middle Ages begin.

5 SECONDS BEFORE MIDNIGHT
The Middle Ages end.

3 SECONDS BEFORE MIDNIGHT
The Pilgrims land in the New World.

1.5 SECONDS BEFORE MIDNIGHT
The Industrial Age begins.

1 SECOND BEFORE MIDNIGHT
The U.S. Civil War begins.

1/2 SECOND BEFORE MIDNIGHT
WWI breaks out.

3/8 SECOND BEFORE MIDNIGHT
WWII begins, ushering in the atomic age.

1/8 SECOND BEFORE MIDNIGHT
Neil Armstrong walks on the moon.

1/16 SECOND BEFORE MIDNIGHT
The computer age begins.

1/32 SECOND BEFORE MIDNIGHT
The age of artificial intelligence and virtual reality follow.

1/64 SECOND BEFORE MIDNIGHT
Humans begin to realize that their activities, begun less than one second ago on the cosmic timetable, have dramatically altered the ecological balance of the planet. At no time in Earth's history has a species had such an impact. What could that mean for the future of Earth?

30,000 B.C. MOON PHASES
Early people carve lines on animal bones to track the phases of the moon.

2500 B.C. STONEHENGE
Stonehenge is built in Britain. The circle of stones marks the rising and setting points of the sun at the summer and winter solstices.

1300 B.C. CONSTELLATIONS AND PLANETS
Egyptians keep track of 43 constellations and the five visible planets—Mars, Venus, Mercury, Jupiter, and Saturn.

350 B.C. SPHERICAL EARTH
Greek scientist Aristotle argues that Earth is a sphere—not flat as believed before—because its shadow on the moon during a lunar eclipse is always a circle.

250 B.C. EARTH'S CIRCUMFERENCE
Greek mathematician Eratosthenes uses geometry to calculate the circumference of Earth—almost 25,000 miles (40,234 km).

150 B.C. EARTH-CENTERED UNIVERSE
Greek astronomer Ptolemy publishes the *Almagest,* an astronomy book that says the universe is centered on Earth.

A.D. 1054 SUPERNOVA
Chinese astronomers record a supernova that is visible in the daytime; the remains of this explosion can now be seen as the Crab Nebula.

1543 SUN-CENTERED SYSTEM
Polish astronomer Nicolaus Copernicus publishes *De Revolutionibus,* which states that the Earth and other planets orbit the sun.

1609 TELESCOPE
Italian astronomer Galileo Galilei uses a telescope to make important observations of the sun, moon, planets, and stars.

1609 PLANETARY MOTION
German mathematician Johannes Kepler discovers the laws of planetary motion, which describe the shape and speed of planetary orbits.

1665–7 GRAVITY
British scientist Isaac Newton discovers the law of universal gravitation.

1781 URANUS
German-born English astronomer William Herschel discovers Uranus, the first planet that had not been known by the ancients.

1846 NEPTUNE
German astronomer Johann Galle discovers the planet Neptune, using calculations from British mathematician John Couch Adams and French astronomer Urbain Le Verrier.

1912 SCALE OF THE UNIVERSE
U.S. astronomer Henrietta Leavitt catalogues the relative brightness and variability of stars. Her work helps astronomers develop a way to calibrate the scale of the universe.

1915 RELATIVITY
German-born physicist Albert Einstein publishes his general theory of relativity, which explains how space curves around matter.

1923 GALAXIES
U.S. astronomer Edwin Hubble shows that spiral nebulas are galaxies—huge collections of stars far from the Milky Way.

1929 EXPANDING UNIVERSE
Edwin Hubble discovers that galaxies are moving apart, because the universe is expanding.

1930 PLUTO
U.S. astronomer Clyde Tombaugh discovers Pluto by spotting a moving speck of light in two photographs of the night sky taken a week apart.

1950 OORT CLOUD
Dutch astronomer Jan Oort says that certain comets come from a band of distant icy objects orbiting the sun, now called the Oort cloud.

1951 KUIPER BELT
U.S. astronomer Gerard Kuiper proposes the existence of a ring of small, icy bodies orbiting just beyond Neptune, now called the Kuiper belt.

1957 SPUTNIK 1
The first man-made satellite, the Soviet Union's Sputnik 1, is launched.

1958 EXPLORER 1
Explorer 1 is the first satellite successfully launched by the United States.

1961 FIRST PEOPLE IN SPACE
Soviet cosmonaut Yuri Gagarin is the first person in space. Astronaut Alan Shepard is the first American in space.

1963 FIRST WOMAN IN SPACE; QUASARS
Soviet cosmonaut Valentina Tereshkova is the first woman in space. Dutch-born U.S. astronomer Maarten Schmidt discovers the first quasar, an extremely bright celestial body.

1965 BIG BANG; MARINER 4
U.S. astronomers Arno Penzias and Robert Wilson use a radio telescope to detect very faint radiation coming from all directions in space. They realize this is radiation left over from the big bang, which helps prove that theory for the formation of the universe. Mariner 4 flies past Mars, sending back pictures of a dry, cratered surface.

1967 PULSARS
British astronomers Jocelyn Bell and Antony Hewish discover pulsars, later shown to be spinning neutron stars sending out beams of radiation.

1969 FIRST PEOPLE ON THE MOON; SOYUZ SPACE STATION
U.S. astronauts Edwin "Buzz" Aldrin and Neil Armstrong become the first people to land on the moon. Soviet spacecraft Soyuz 5 docks with Soyuz 4 to form the first experimental space station.

1972 LAST MOON LANDING
Apollo 17 is the last Apollo mission to the moon.

1976 VIKING LANDERS
U.S. Viking landers safely touch down on the surface of Mars and send back images and information from the planet's surface for several years.

1979 VOYAGERS 1 AND 2
U.S. spacecraft Voyagers 1 and 2 reach Jupiter, then use gravitational assists from their swing past Jupiter to speed toward the more-distant planets.

1981 SPACE SHUTTLE LAUNCHED
U.S. space shuttle *Columbia* is launched, successfully making the first flight of a reusable shuttle.

1986 *CHALLENGER* DISASTER; MIR 1
The space shuttle *Challenger* explodes 73 seconds after launch, killing the crew. Soviets launch the space station Mir 1.

1989 COBE
The Cosmic Background Explorer (COBE) satellite is launched. It detects microwave radiation in the universe that confirms modern theories about the big bang.

1990 MAGELLAN; HUBBLE SPACE TELESCOPE
U.S. spacecraft Magellan begins radar mapping of Venus. The Hubble Space Telescope is launched. In the years to come, it produces stunning images of distant stars and galaxies.

1992 KUIPER BELT OBJECT
Astronomers discover a reddish, planetlike object circling the sun beyond the orbit of Pluto, confirming the existence of the Kuiper belt.

1995 PLANETS ORBITING OTHER STARS
Jupiter-size planets are discovered orbiting sunlike stars near our solar system in the Milky Way.

2003 *COLUMBIA* DISASTER
After 27 missions, the space shuttle *Columbia* explodes during reentry into Earth's atmosphere, killing all aboard.

2004 MARS ROVERS; CASSINI
U.S. rovers Spirit and Opportunity reach Mars and begin collecting information about the existence of water. The U.S. Cassini spacecraft goes into orbit around Saturn, sending back images of the planet, its rings, and its large moon Titan.

2004 ERIS
Eris, a planetlike object bigger than Pluto, is first seen orbiting the sun more than six billion miles (10 billion km) away, far past Pluto.

2006 PLUTO DEMOTED
Members of the International Astronomical Union vote to change the way planets are classified. Pluto is no longer considered a planet but officially becomes a dwarf planet, along with Eris and Ceres (formerly the solar system's biggest asteroid).

2012 CURIOSITY ROVER
NASA launches the Curiosity Rover in November 2011, and it lands on the Gale Crater on Mars in August 2012. Its goal is to study the climate and geology of the crater to figure out if it has ever supported microbial life.

2015 PLUTO FLYBY
The U.S. New Horizons spacecraft will fly past Pluto on its way to the farthest reaches of the solar system.

2018 HUBBLE REPLACEMENT
The James Webb Space Telescope will be launched to replace the Hubble Space Telescope.

ASTEROID
A rocky body, measuring from less than one mile to 600 miles (1.6 to 966 km) in diameter, in orbit around a sun. Most asteroids in our solar system are found between the orbits of Mars and Jupiter.

ATMOSPHERE
The gases surrounding a planet, star, or satellite

BIG BANG
An enormous explosion that scientists believe was the initial event in the formation of the universe

BLACK DWARF
The cooling remains of a dwarf star that has used up its nuclear fuel

BLACK HOLE
Thought to form when a massive star collapses. Black holes are extremely dense objects of such strong gravitational force that nothing passing within a certain distance can escape them, not even light.

BROWN DWARF
A faintly glowing body too small to sustain a nuclear fusion reaction and become a star

COMET
A body of rock, dust, and gaseous ice in an elongated orbit around the sun. Near the sun, heat diffuses gas and dust to form a streaming "tail" around the comet's nucleus.

CONSTELLATION
A pattern of stars identified with an ancient god, goddess, or animal; also an area of sky with one of these star patterns

CORONA
The outermost layer of gases in the sun's atmosphere

CRATER
A circular depression in the surface of a planet, caused by a meteorite impact or by volcanic action

DARK MATTER
An unknown substance that is only detectable by the gravity it exerts. It makes up 23 percent of the universe.

DWARF PLANET
A spherical or nearly spherical rocky body in orbit around the sun and not the satellite of another body; smaller than most of the other planets in our solar system

ECLIPSE
An event caused by the passage of one astronomical body between an observer and another astronomical body, briefly blocking light from the farther astronomical body

FISSION
The breakdown of atomic nuclei into the nuclei of lighter elements, releasing energy

FUSION
The combining of the nuclei of two atoms to form one, heavier nucleus, a process that releases energy

GALAXY
A grouping of stars, gas, and dust bound together by gravity. Galaxies sometimes have many billions of stars.

GAMMA-RAY BURST
A brief, intense burst of gamma radiation. These are the brightest explosions in the universe and come from sources outside our galaxy.

KUIPER BELT
A reservoir of comets encircling an area just beyond the orbit of Neptune

LIGHT-YEAR
Equals six trillion miles (ten trillion km), the distance light can travel in one Earth year

MAGNITUDE
A number measuring an astronomical body's brightness in relation to other luminous objects

MASS
The total quantity of material in an object, determining its gravity and resistance to movement

METEOR
A small object from space that appears as a streak of light when it passes through Earth's atmosphere. A meteorite is the remains of a meteor found on Earth. A meteoroid is a rocky or metallic object in orbit around the sun that has the potential to become a meteor.

NEBULA
A glowing interstellar cloud of gas and dust

NEUTRON STAR
A body of densely packed neutrons formed after the explosion of a supernova. A neutron star only ten miles (16 km) in diameter could have more mass than three sun-size stars.

OORT CLOUD
A reservoir of comets surrounding our solar system

ORBIT
The regular path a celestial body follows as it revolves around another body

PLANET
A spherical object larger than 600 miles (966 km) in diameter that orbits a star and has cleared its neighborhood of other like-size objects

PLANETARY NEBULA
The glowing cloud of gas resulting from a supernova explosion

PLANETESIMAL
A small rocky body in orbit around a star, which may become a planet by drawing in more material

PULSAR
Thought to be a spinning neutron star that sends out bursts of electromagnetic radiation with clockwork regularity

RED GIANT
A cool, aging low-mass star that has fused most of its core hydrogen and expanded greatly from its previous size

RING
A band of material around a planet, formed of dust-to-boulder-size pieces

SATELLITE
A natural or man-made object orbiting a planet

SOLAR (STELLAR) WIND
A stream of charged particles radiating outward from the sun or another star

SPECTRUM
The range of radiation wavelengths from long radio waves to short gamma rays. The visible portion can be seen as colors when the radiation (light) is passed through a prism.

SUPERGIANT
A very massive, luminous star with a relatively short life span

SUPERNOVA
The violent, luminous explosion at the end of a massive star's life

WHITE DWARF
The small, dense core of a once larger star that has fused all the helium in its core

DAVID A. AGUILAR is a naturalist, astronomer, and astronomical artist with a passion for bringing the wonders of space to wider audiences. He is the director of public affairs and science information at the Harvard-Smithsonian Center for Astrophysics in Cambridge, Massachusetts, the world's largest astronomical research organization. He also leads world tours for Smithsonian and Harvard. David is the author and illustrator of six National Geographic books and the originator of the Science Discovery Program at the University of Colorado, in Boulder. He was marketing director for the Emmy-winning seven-part PBS NOVA series *Evolution*. David has appeared the "Alien Faces" episode of the History channel's *The Universe*, as well as UFO Hunters, and the Weather Channel's 2013 series *Planet Earth*. His artwork has been featured in *Time* magazine, *US News & World Report*, the *New York Times, USA Today, Sky & Telescope, Astronomy* magazine, and *Scientific American*, and on CNN, the BBC, and the nightly news on ABC, CBS, and NBC. David can be contacted at www.aspenskies.com.

CHRISTINE PULLIAM, contributing writer ("To the Stars & Beyond"), is a public affairs specialist at the Harvard-Smithsonian Center for Astrophysics in Cambridge, Massachusetts, and a freelance science writer. She earned her B.S. in physics and her M.A. in astronomy from the University of Texas at Austin.

PATRICIA DANIELS, contributing writer ("Dreams of Tomorrow" and time lines of the solar system and astronomy), has written more than a dozen science and history books for adults and children, including the *National Geographic Encyclopedia of Space* and *Constellations: My First Pocket Guide*. She lives in State College, Pennsylvania.

All illustrations and images courtesy of David A. Aguilar unless otherwise noted.

10–11, NASA; 30 (UP LE), NASA; 30–31 (LO), NASA; 38 (UP LE), NASA; 38 (LE CTR), NASA; 42 (UP RT), NASA; 43 (UP), NASA; 43 (CTR), NASA; 50 (UP), Wikipedia; 51 (UP RT), NASA; 51 (LO CTR), NASA; (UP LE), NASA; 52 (UP RT), NASA; 53 (UP LE), NASA; 53 (UP RT), NASA; 56–57, NASA; 58 (LE), NASA; 58 (RT), NASA; 59 (CTR LE), NASA; 59 (LO), NASA; 59 (UP), NASA; 68 (LE), Clyde Tombaugh/Corbis; 86–87 Shutterstock, except 87 (UP LE), Douglas P. Wilson/Frank Lane Picture Agency/Corbis; 94–95, Serge Brunier; 96 (LO), art info/The Bridgeman Art Library; 102–103, NASA/JPL; 103 (INSET), NASA; 106 (UP), Robert Gendler/www.robgendlerastropics.com; 106 (LO), Robert Gendler/www .robgendlerastropics.com; 107 (UP LE), painting by Thomas Shotter Boys/Eileen Tweedy/The Art Archive at Art Resource, NY; 107 (UP RT), Wikipedia; 110, NASA/SOHO; 111 (UP), Robert Gendler/www.robgendlerastropics .com; 111 (CTR), Robert Gendler/ www.robgendlerastropics.com; 111 (LO), Bruce Balick/NASA; 114 (LO LE), NASA; 117 (RT CTR), Envision/CORBIS; 132 Ted Spiegel; 133 (CTR), Robert Gendler/www.robgendlerastropics .com; 133 (LO), NOAO/AURA/ NSF; 138 (LE), NASA/GSFC; 138 (UP RT), NASA/GSFC; 138 (LO RT), NASA/Kirk Borne/ STScI; 139 (LO LE), NASA/EJ Schreie/STScI; 144, NASA; 145 (RT), NASA; 172 (UP), NASA; 178, NASA

Baumann, Mary K., Will Hopkins, Loralee Nolletti, and Michael Soluri. *What's Out There: Images from Here to the Edge of the Universe*. London: Duncan Baird, 2006.

Beatty, J. Kelly, Carolyn Petersen, and Andrew Chaikin, Ed. *The New Solar System*. Cambridge, Mass.: Sky Publishing, 1999.

Crelin, Bob. *There Once Was a Sky Full of Stars*. Cambridge, Mass.: Sky Publishing, 2007.

Croswell, Ken. *Ten Worlds: Everything That Orbits the Sun*. Honesdale, Pa.: Boyds Mills Press, 2006.

Darling, David. *The Universal Book of Astronomy*. Hoboken, N.J.: Wiley, 2004.

Davis, Kenneth C. *Don't Know Much About Space*. New York: HarperCollins, 2001.

Decristofano, Carolyn Cinami, and Michael Carroll. *Big Bang!* Watertown, Mass.: Charlesbridge Publishing, 2005.

Dinwiddie, Robert et al. *Universe*. New York: Dorling Kindersley, 2005.

Glover, Linda, et al. *National Geographic Encyclopedia of Space*. Washington, D.C.: National Geographic Society, 2005.

Harrington, Philip, and Edward Pascuzzi. *Astronomy for All Ages*. Old Saybrook, Conn.: Globe Pequot, 2000.

Hewitt-White, Ken. *Patterns in the Sky*. Cambridge, Mass.: Sky Publishing, 2007.

Odenwald, Sten. *Back to Astronomy Café*. Boulder, Colo.: Westview Press, 2003.

Schorer, Lonnie. *Kids to Space: A Space Traveler's Guide*. Burlington, Ontario: Collector's Guide Publishing, Inc., 2006.

Skurzynski, Gloria. *Are We Alone?* Washington, D.C.: National Geographic Society, 2004.

Time-Life Books, Ed. *Comets, Asteroids, and Meteorites*. Alexandria, Va.: Time-Life, Inc., 1990.

Villard, Ray, and Lynette Cook. *Infinite Worlds*. Berkeley: University of California Press, 2005.

WEBSITES

To learn more about space and astronomy, check out these websites.

antwrp.gsfc.nasa.gov/apod/astropix.html

www.astronomycafe.net

www.chandra.harvard.edu

www.hubblesite.org

imagine.gsfc.nasa.gov/docs/ask_astro/ask_an_astronomer.html

www.kidsastronomy.com

www.nasa.gov/centers/goddard/home/index.html

www.nineplanets.org

www.space.com/science-astronomy

PUBLISHED BY THE NATIONAL GEOGRAPHIC SOCIETY

John M. Fahey, *Chairman of the Board and
Chief Executive Officer*

Declan Moore, *Executive Vice President;
President, Publishing and Travel*

Melina Gerosa Bellows, *Executive Vice
President; Chief Creative Officer,
Books, Kids, and Family*

PREPARED BY THE BOOK DIVISION

Hector Sierra, *Senior Vice President and
General Manager*

Nancy Laties Feresten, *Senior Vice
President, Kids Publishing and Media*

Jay Sumner, *Director of Photography,
Children's Publishing*

Jennifer Emmett, *Vice President, Editorial
Director, Children's Books*

Eva Absher-Schantz, *Design Director,
Kids Publishing and Media*

R. Gary Colbert, *Production Director*

Jennifer A. Thornton, *Director of
Managing Editorial*

STAFF FOR THIS BOOK

Priyanka Lamichhane, *Project Editor*

David M. Seager, *Art Director*

Lori Epstein, *Senior Illustrations Editor*

Ariane Szu-Tu, *Editorial Assistant*

Callie Broaddus,
Design Production Assistant

Hillary Moloney, *Illustrations Assistant*

Patricia Daniels, *Contributing Writer*

Julie Beer, Michelle R. Harris, *Researchers*

Grace Hill, *Associate Managing Editor*

Joan Gossett, *Production Editor*

Lewis R. Bassford, *Production Manager*

Susan Borke, *Legal and Business Affairs*

MANUFACTURING AND QUALITY MANAGEMENT

Phillip L. Schlosser, *Senior Vice President*

Chris Brown, *Vice President, NG Book
Manufacturing*

George Bounelis, *Vice President,
Production Services*

Nicole Elliott, *Manager*

Rachel Faulise, *Manager*

Robert L. Barr, *Manager*

This book is dedicated to James Gordon Irving, illustrator of *Stars*
and other Golden Nature Guide books, who first inspired me to try oil
painting the solar system while in junior high school;
to Chesley Bonestell, mentor, friend, and visionary of the future
conquest of space; to Arthur C. Clarke, Isaac Asimov, and Carl Sagan,
who enlightened and lit the fires of imagination with their beautifully
written books about space and science fiction.

Lastly, this book would not have been possible without the
loving insights, laughter, and support of my wife Shirley, "Queen of the
Asteroids," and the unwavering drive and monumentally gifted artistic
talents of David M. Seager, the book's art director.
Their passions for the beauty and mysteries of space are in
every piece of art work found in this book.

DAVID A. AGUILAR

CELEBRATING
‹125›
YEARS

The National Geographic Society is one of the world's largest nonprofit scientific and educational
organizations. Founded in 1888 to "increase and diffuse geographic knowledge," the Society's
mission is to inspire people to care about the planet. It reaches more than 400 million people
worldwide each month through its official journal, *National Geographic,* and other magazines;
National Geographic Channel; television documentaries; music; radio; films; books; DVDs; maps;
exhibitions; live events; school publishing programs; interactive media; and merchandise. National
Geographic has funded more than 10,000 scientific research, conservation and exploration projects
and supports an education program promoting geographic literacy.

For more information, please visit www.nationalgeographic.com,
call 1-800-NGS LINE (647-5463), or write to the following address:
National Geographic Society
1145 17th Street N.W.
Washington, D.C. 20036-4688 U.S.A.

Visit us online at www.nationalgeographic.com/books

For librarians and teachers: www.ngchildrensbooks.org

More for kids from National Geographic: kids.nationalgeographic.com

For information about special discounts for bulk purchases, please contact National Geographic
Books Special Sales: ngspecsales@ngs.org

For rights or permissions inquiries, please contact National Geographic Books Subsidiary Rights:
ngbookrights@ngs.org

Hardcover ISBN: 978-1-4263-0948-9
Reinforced Library Binding ISBN: 978-1-4263-1560-2
Scholastic ISBN: 978-1-4263-1629-6

Printed in China
13/CCOS/1